ITALIANS
OF THE
NORTH END

ITALIANS
OF THE
NORTH END

*A History of Grit,
Perseverance & Tradition*

PATRICIA M. ANNINO

THE
History
PRESS

Published by The History Press
Charleston, SC
www.historypress.com

First published 2024

Manufactured in the United States

ISBN 9781467155403

Library of Congress Control Number: 2023947107

Notice: The information in this book is true and complete to the best of our knowledge. It is offered without guarantee on the part of the author or The History Press. The author and The History Press disclaim all liability in connection with the use of this book.

This book is dedicated to my grandparents Anthony Annino and Elvira Gaeta Annino and their children, Kathryn (Annino) D'Andraia, Anthony Annino, Dorothy (Annino) Iseman and my father, Donald J. Annino.

CONTENTS

PREFACE

Last year, I walked through the North End and appreciated its narrow streets in a different way than I had before. I am half Italian and half Irish. The North End has always seemed familiar to me, although no one in my family lived there at any time in my life. It is familiar because it was and is the essence of being Italian—the restaurants, the bakeries, the streets, the men sitting on chairs on the sidewalk talking to the passersby, the regulars who meet in the coffee shops each morning on Hanover Street, the Catholic Mass in both Italian and English at St. Leonard's Church. The North End has the warm feeling of a protected enclave steeped in culture and history. I have always been aware that beneath that veneer there is more than a century of evolution—hardship, discrimination, persistence, perseverance, connection to the past and pushing into the future.

What exactly is the story of the Italians in the North End? Is it what it appeared to me to be? How did it happen? Can it last? Why does it matter? Those questions are what compelled me to spend a year of Saturdays in the North End library searching for answers and writing this book.

I hope that you will enjoy it as much as I enjoyed the journey of researching and writing it.

ACKNOWLEDGEMENTS

A heartfelt thank-you to Linda Cashdan for her review and editing of the manuscript; my cousin Frank D'Andraia for his review of the manuscript, his wisdom and his devotion to our family heritage; my husband, Robert Carr, for the many conversations on topics and observations; my niece Grace Annino for her strategic input; and Ashley Kaitz for her thorough research.

Thanks also to the North End scholars, historians and authors who created and contributed to significant bodies of work that are the backbone of this book: Robert J. Allinson, Alex Goldfield, William DeMarco, Augusto Ferraiuolo, James Pasto, Stephen Puleo, Jessica Dello Russo, the late Anthony Riccio, Anthony Sammarco and Paula Todisco.

Thanks to those in the North End who were kind enough to speak with me and give their thoughts and perspectives, especially Claudia Carroll, Father Michael Della Penna, Anthony Gambale, Thomas Damigella, Jessica Dello Russo, Marilyn and Joseph Frissora, Doreen Merola, Bennett Molinari, Richard Molinari and Maria Russo. Thank you to Eleni and IAM Bookstore for pointing me in the right direction and highlighting excellent resources.

Special thanks to Vito Aluia, Thomas Damigella and the North End Historical Society for the lending of the photographs in this book

1

EMIGRATION FROM ITALY

People who leave their own country for another country do so usually because they
are dissatisfied with their lot in their native land, and hope to secure a greater
measure of happiness under the flag of some other nation.
—George Scigliano, 1903

The only person who leaves his native country is a person who has been
abandoned by it. Here, I found my dignity and self-esteem. At least in America
you can dream. Everything starts with a dream.
Freedom is the realization of your dream.
—Les Marino, founder, Modern Continental Company, August 2000

Imagine you are a strapping twenty-year-old man in excellent health in
southern Italy in 1900. There is no future for you in your village, in any
neighboring village or in southern Italy as a whole. You and all your
compadres are peasant farmers and illiterate. You do not have any other job
skills. You do not want to leave your native country, your family and your
friends, but you must.

That's because Italy has changed dramatically. Taxes have skyrocketed.
Natural disasters have taken hold. The confluence of these events has
robbed you and your family of the ability to make a living. Your family and
neighbors have been pushed to the brink of starvation. You have no hope.

UNIFICATION OF ITALY FROM MANY KINGDOMS TO ONE

Until 1861, there was no Italy as we think of it now. Between the fall of the Roman empire in AD 476 and the period of unification (also known as the Risorgimento), Italy consisted of separate kingdoms and papal territories. It was a collection of city-states. From 1859 to 1861, most of Italy (except Veneto and the Vatican) unified into a single state—the Kingdom of Italy. The unification was not peaceful. It was the outcome of war among kingdoms within Italy.

The period of unification (1861–71) did not wave a magic wand. The people were by no means unified. Unification did not provide a common identity for those who had believed themselves for centuries to be different from one another. Throughout the years, the people in Italy had defined themselves not as one country, but as part of much smaller entities, associating themselves primarily with their parents, their families, their immediate neighbors and their villages. There was no sense of nationalism. There was no national pride in being Italian; the allegiance was strictly local. The significant difference between northern Italy (industrial) and southern Italy (agrarian) caused economic and political resentments.[1]

Massimo d'Azeglio, the prime minister of Sardinia, is famous for this statement: "We have made Italy, now we have to make Italians." (Ironically, most did not identify as Italian until they came to America and found strength with other Italians fighting economic hardship and discrimination.)[2]

Financial Pressures

The unification of Italian states into the Kingdom of Italy necessitated changes in governmental structure. This change in the government's organization changed Italy. Unifying was not a simple, quick or inexpensive process. In 1865, Italy adopted a new civil code. The right of succession to a specific parcel of property was abolished. Ownership of land became fragmented. This did not help the southern Italians. Many southern Italians remained without landownership. The lots of land that did exist were broken up and made smaller. Landowners in southern Italy had to face increasing fiscal pressure from the government, which was engaged in the construction of infrastructure for the newly created Kingdom of Italy.

After unification, the government imposed a heavy tariff on the rural manufacture of silk (which had already been damaged by the silkworm disease of 1856–63). This opened the door for competition from British silk producers.

The economic pressures continued through the 1800s. In the late 1870s, the Italian government heavily taxed wheat (which had already fallen to a record low price) and salt (which was widely used as a preservative). The Italian government forced the southern Italian peasants to pay upward of 90 percent of their crops in taxes. The taxes in Italy were the highest in Europe and weighed heavily on those who had the least ability to pay—the *contadini* (peasants) and the *giarnalieri* (day laborers). Excise taxes were placed on salt, sugar, tobacco, liquor, flour, bread and macaroni—all items over which the Italian government had a monopoly. In addition to the Italian tax, there were also taxes imposed by the provinces and communities. These taxes led to financial destruction.

The financial pressure did not help the relationship between the southern Italian peasants and the Catholic Church. While the peasant farmers were paying exorbitant taxes and struggling to survive, the clergy still received salaries from the government. It appeared to the peasants that the priests did not suffer economically and still maintained their reasonably comfortable lifestyle. This caused suspicion, and with that suspicion came religious indifference.

Northern-Southern Hostility

The unification did not soften the centuries of hostility between the northerners (those from Rome, Venice, Piedmont and Genoa) and southerners (those from Avellino, Calabria, Abruzzi and Sicily). Northern Italians continued to disparage their southern counterparts, considering them primitive. This prejudice had racial overtones. The northern Italians were Germanic and French. The southern Italians were descendants of Greeks, Turks and Africans. Northern Italians were considered cosmopolitan, educated and financially secure. Southern Italians were characterized as parochial, illiterate peasant farmers. (Later, these feelings carried over to Boston, when both northern and southern Italians immigrated there and lived together in the North End).

Abundance of Natural Disasters

In the 1800s, Italy had more than its share of natural disasters. In 1880, in the province of Avellino, virtually all of the crops suffered from disease. Absentee landlords who lived in northern Italy expected the peasant farmers in southern Italy to absorb the financial loss. In 1881, bread riots broke out when nearly 65 percent of the Naples-Avellino population was without work. In 1882, a cholera epidemic broke out in Naples. In the late 1890s, the citrus crop (a source of pride for Campania and Sicily) suffered poor harvests in a row, due to drought and diseased trees, enabling the U.S. citrus industry to gain a toehold in the world market. Similar conditions destroyed vineyards. This allowed the French vineyards to gain inroads into an industry that Italy had dominated in Europe. In 1905, earthquakes in Calabria and Basilicata killed 30,000. In 1906, Mount Vesuvius erupted, burying towns near Naples. In 1908, an earthquake devastated Messina in Sicily, killing more than 100,000 people. In 1910, Mount Etna erupted in Sicily, killing more than 10,000.

Rising Birth Rates

To top it off, during this time, in spite of all the crushing economic pressures and natural disasters, the birth rate in Italy rose dramatically. In the late nineteenth century, Italy was the fourth-most densely populated country in Europe. The population grew substantially from 18 million in 1801 to 32 million in 1901. Overpopulation and overcrowding in an economically fragile area contributed to the problems at hand.

THE GRAND EMIGRATION

Our peasants are in worse condition than the serfs of the Middle Ages. The landlords treat them like slaves. Peasants live like beasts. Their sense of dignity seems to have died centuries ago. They have two equally hard choices before them—submission and work until an untimely death or rebellion and a violent death—unless they are willing to escape to somewhere else.[3]

And so, between 1880 and 1930, more than 17 million Italians left Italy. Many of them were southern Italians. This migration was not just to the

United States. It was also to France, Switzerland, Brazil and Argentina. With improved maritime transportation, emigration became easier. Cruise lines opened agencies in Italy, creating a web of agents and relations aimed at encouraging and publicizing the perspective of migration to America.

Early in the first decade of the twentieth century, a story was told in Italy of a trip made by Italian prime minister Giuseppe Zanardelli through one of the southern provinces that had experienced heavy emigration. The mayor and chief men of one town, Moiterno, met the minister at the train and escorted him to the central square, where an enthusiastic crowd greeted him. The mayor mounted a platform that had been built for the occasion, looked down on the crowd and delivered welcoming remarks to the prime minister: "I welcome you in the name of 5,000 inhabitants of this town—3,000 of whom are in America and the other 2,000 of them preparing to go."[4]

Italy encouraged the emigration. In 1888, the Italian government passed a law approving the complete liberty to emigrate. The Italian government considered emigration a necessary tool to control the social unrest because it was the unemployed and impoverished members of the working class who were leaving the country. Emigration provided a safety valve to the overcrowding and poverty-stricken conditions in Italy. The Italian government was also very much aware that those who emigrated sent money back to their families in Italy, and that money was an important resource for the Italian economy. The Italian government cooperated with the United States in keeping criminals from emigrating and trying to make sure that most people emigrating were healthy. This concern over the "quality" of the emigrant had benefits. Compared to nationals from any other immigrant group, Italians had the lowest percent of rejections on landing in the United States.

The Catholic Church supported the Italian emigration. Fearing that emigration was going to incur loss of the faithful forever in favor of Protestant churches, however, the Catholic Church reacted and organized associations and parishes for the Italians abroad.[5]

Birds of Passage: Earn and Return

Leaving their family, friends, village and native country was difficult. Return migration occurred. Some of the southern Italians became "birds of passage"—those who came to America to work seasonally and then returned to Italy in the winter (known as "earn and return").[6]

It was difficult for many emigrants to leave their families and their country. Just as startling is the percentage of Italians who, despite the brutal conditions in southern Italy, decided before they left Italy that they would return to Italy.[7]

As many as 1.5 million emigrants eventually returned to Italy permanently between 1910 and 1914. Many of the emigrants had left their peasant villages, where they had been making their living through farming, raising livestock or growing fruit trees, and settled in Boston and other cities in America, where they lived in crowded tenements, not farmlands with fresh air. Not all were able to bridge the cultural gap between the peasant life they knew in Italy and the fast-paced life and culture in America.

CULTURE SHOCK

Culture shock is the experience of entering a foreign culture and discovering you can neither communicate your thoughts to others nor understand their thoughts. The barriers to communication went far beyond language. They included differences in customs, outlooks on life, types of emotional expression and body language. These were real obstacles the immigrants encountered. The love of family and homeland turned out to be a powerful force. It is startling how many Italians, despite the brutal conditions in southern Italy, apparently decided they would return to Italy *before* leaving Italy. This decision was based on an economic plan. Once they achieved their financial goal, they would return to Italy. The returnees were, for the most part, neither rejected by American society nor spurred on by nostalgia. Rather they were individuals actively pursuing goals they had set before departure.[8]

As Giovanni Iorenzano, a student of migration in Italy, wrote in the 1870s, "Our emigrants carry their mother country in their hearts and maintain a political tie with it, and they return as soon as they have put together a small nest egg. In this respect they are different from the English, Irish, and Germans who go to America to become citizens."[9]

Those who persevered and remained in America achieved economic stability and cultural exposure that would have made it difficult to return to the Italy they left and be comfortable there.

As A. Bartlett Giamatti, former president of Yale University, wrote,

> *Once the immigrants had seen America, they were spoiled forever because they knew a fantastic, open secret: even life tough and demanding in a strange world can change. Change is possible. Change is America. America was a place which was not like Italy, the Italy that was ever the same, shaped by fate, burdened by history. In America there was a chance for change. That story went back and millions came. The American dream became the dream of the land of change. It was the first dream not fated.... It was itself, like America, a new thing.*[10]

2

IMMIGRATION AND ITS CHALLENGES

Let us welcome all immigrants who are sound mentally and physically and intelligent and let us protect the country from those who tend to lower the average of health and intelligence.
—*Prescott Hall, 1907*

The Puritan is passed; the Anglo-Saxon is a joke:
A newer and better America is here.
—*James Michael Curley, 1916*

THE JOURNEY TO AMERICA

Deciding to leave Italy was a decision Italians did not take lightly. Stories of how difficult the passage would be were well known. Coming to America was a difficult journey fraught with peril and uncertainty. Family mattered most. Hope and resilience were important, as there was little else to rely on.

By the late 1890s, twelve to fourteen steamship companies offered direct service between Naples, Italy, and New York City. Life in steerage was grim, lasting from two weeks to a month. Conditions were crowded, filthy and uncomfortable. Lice, scurvy and seasickness added to the passengers' misery. The passage to America was difficult and dangerous.[11] On March 18, 1891, the SS *Utopia*, en route from Trieste, Italy, to New York City's Ellis Island,

Italian men at Ellis Island awaiting immigration. *Boston Public Library*.

with stops in Naples, Genoa and Gibraltar, sank in Gibraltar Bay within twenty minutes of colliding with the Royal Navy warship HMS *Anson*, which was at anchor. The weather was terrible. On board *Utopia* were 880 passengers and crew. Most were Italian immigrants. More than 500 died. Some of the survivors were so scared they decide to return to Italy and never again brave the dangers of an ocean voyage.[12]

Immigrants traveled to the ships (mostly departing from Naples) by whatever means available—train, bus, horse and carriage. They underwent humiliating fumigation of their bodies, clothes and goods; a document verification; and then a cursory medical exam. Steerage was in the bottom of the boat. The steerage "halls" were lined with rows of metal bunks stacked two high. There was no privacy. The bedding consisted of straw mattresses with a piece of canvas sheeting. A life preserver was their pillow. They were given a lightweight blanket and a set of metal eating utensils—fork, spoon and tin lunch pail. Italians brought along knapsacks of cheese and salami to supplement the inedible soup provided by the steamship company.

There were no dining tables or chairs. The stench of vomit and urine was prevalent, with little ventilation.

While on board, those who could read studied books "guaranteed" to teach English within the time of the voyage. Others consulted guidebooks that explained America.

When they landed at Ellis Island, their primary concern was getting through the medical exam. Chalk marks on the clothes of an immigrant identified a medical condition:

H—for heart problems
E—for eye problems
L—for lameness

The United States also required an intelligence exam to identify the "idiots, imbeciles, morons or other mentally deficient persons." Those with minor illnesses were held in quarantine for a day or so. Those with severe medical conditions were put aside and deported back to Italy.

For these reasons, the Italians dubbed Ellis Island L'Isola Dell Langrime—"the island of tears."[13]

The Saint Raphael Society for the Protection of Italian Immigrants helped Italian immigrants arriving at Ellis Island through the process to avoid deportation.

Very few Italian immigrants entered America through Boston. More than 15,000 Italians were processed daily at Ellis Island, the port of entry for 97 percent of the Italians seeking to immigrate. From 1891 to 1900, 651,893 Italians arrived; from 1901 to 1910, 2 million arrived. The Boston Italian population swelled from 4,700 in 1890 to 13,700 by 1900 and 31,380 by 1910.[14]

THE PADRONE SYSTEM

The Italian government was criticized in the United States for the role it played in working with shipping companies to encourage emigration to relieve the economic pressure in Italy. The average Italian immigrant during this time arrived in America with thirteen to seventeen dollars. Once in America, Italian immigrants—most of whom were illiterate in their native language—were often besieged by unscrupulous opportunists looking to cheat them out of the meager money they had brought with them from Italy. These included padroni or labor contractors who would make promises about work they would not keep. Unscrupulous padroni extorted exorbitant fees from unsuspecting immigrants, held back full employment payments for weeks or months and collaborated in rural areas

Italian family at Ellis island. *Boston Public Library.*

with owners of "company" stores, forcing Italians to purchase goods at inflated prices.[15]

The padrone system had two major labor agents in Boston: the Torchia Company and Stabile and Company. Both worked closely with White Star Shipping Lines, which had direct weekly passenger arrivals to the port of Boston through Naples and Genoa. These agencies provided Boston factories with Neapolitan and other southern Italian manpower through a series of contacts that extended all the way to the villages of southern Italy. Passage of employment was provided in return for a year of employment with the contracting firm.[16]

In the book *Voices of Ellis Island: An Italian American Odyssey*, Anthony Amore told his own story after he immigrated to the North End of Boston in 1902:

> *In the early days Antonio would often go to North Square where the padrones would come to hire him for the day. Padroni were the bosses who hired Italian labor. The term was originally part of the class system in rural Italy. In America the use of the word continued, although the system functioned differently. What remained the same was the laborer was still beholden to the boss. Some of the padroni really looked after their less fortunate countrymen, setting up apartments and jobs for them. Others took advantage of the immigrants' naivete and bound them to doing business in their stores and banks. They would sponsor the passage of young men eager to leave Italy and then require the immigrants to work for low wages in squalid conditions until the loan was repaid. Obtaining a job prior to coming to America could prohibit entrance to the "golden land." This was often a double bind for destitute villagers looking for a way to cross the ocean. If an Ellis Island inspector found that a padrone had sponsored an immigrant, he could be deported back to his country of origin.*[17]

In the book *Boston's North End: Images and Recollections of an Italian-American Neighborhood*, Riccio notes that at the turn of the twentieth century, southern Italy was a harsh, oppressive land that offered its people little hope for improvement, especially day laborers, fishermen and tenant farmers of the poor classes who lived in remote farm regions and small towns where social and economic conditions remained medieval in their backwardness.[18] Many peasant farmers were barely able to provide themselves with life's necessities and chose to leave. From ancient villages with names like Riesi, Sciacca and Salerni, hundreds of thousands of rural folks left for America believing a better life was ahead.

A North Ender, Tom Bardetti, said:

> *My father came here in 1905 because he could not make a living in Italy. Necessity brought him here. In Italy nobody could make it. In those days if you stayed in Italy you wasn't going nowhere. If you wanted to get anywhere, wanted to do anything, you'd have to get out of Italy, you'd have to go to either England or Germany or Australia or some other country*

where you'd have the chance to advance. If you stayed in Italy, you couldn't advance yourself because there was no change there. If you didn't own your own farm to work your own crops you couldn't live….A lot of immigrants had the handicap of not being able to speak the language. So, although they were healthy and strong, they used to do pick and shovel jobs digging. You didn't have to know how to speak the language to do that. And as a laborer, my father didn't know how to speak the language and you're in a foreign country and you don't know how to speak the language, what can you do? You can't do nothing but labor—see?[19]

Riccio pointed out that all the southern Italians wanted was a job. If you ever mentioned welfare to those people, people would cry. Welfare was a dishonor, a disgrace. There was no welfare, no food stamps, no Medicaid, no Medicare, no unemployment benefits, no rent subsidies. The Italian immigrant relied on himself and his family to survive. They were hard workers, and the North End provided them with many opportunities for employment. America was exploding. There were thousands of jobs in construction, wholesale food (meat and producing) and the fishing industry. A short walk or trolley ride away provided additional opportunities for hotels, warehouses, restaurants, taverns and coffee shops.

Charles Polcari, a native North Ender, said:

Sheafe Street, 1920. *Scheslinger Library, Radcliffe Institute, Harvard University.*

When the demand for labor jobs was at its peak, there used to be 400–500 Italian people on North Square waiting for jobs to work out in the country. There used to be contracts for all kinds of trades, and they used to take them (the immigrants) away with them for the whole summer. The immigrants used to say, "We'll stay here and wait for the election. If a Republican comes in we will stay here, we will get work. If a Democrat becomes President we will starve, so we will go back to the old country." This was in 1918 and even before that. But the Irish got jobs because they spoke English. What kind of jobs could the Italians get? There were a lot of smart Italians then but the Irish got the jobs because they could speak English and Italians couldn't. If you didn't know the language what kind of job were they gonna get?[20]

Another North Ender, Fred Bourne, said:

They used to hire immigrant laborers by the day, 50 or 60 guys lined up on Unity Street every morning and they'd pick 10 or 12 of them do go to work for construction jobs. 90% of the jobs were pick and shovel. They worked 10-hour days six days a week for $12. Everyone had to pay a $2.00 "tribute" that went to the boys. There was a fellow—"Tough Tony" was his name. Every week he would come by for your $2.00 and if you did not give it to him you got your legs broken. And one guy who lived in the apartment behind me—a married fella 23 years old from Italy—refused to pay the tribute money. So, one day they shot him on Unity Street. They killed him, which put a sense of fear in all of us.[21]

According to Massachusetts representative George Scigliano, who represented the North End, in almost all cases, payments were held back and never received. The money was not paid to the laborers, so at the end of the season, the laborers returned to the city in the winter with no funds. Loan sharks would offer unsuspecting Italians money at exorbitant interest rates. Often disembarking immigrants were approached by boardinghouse swindlers, and when they arrived at the boardinghouse, there were no available rooms. Scigliano called the padrone system "perhaps the greatest evil which has beset the Italian immigrant in this country."[22] The public and press supported the bill.[23]

PROTECTION FOR THE ITALIAN IMMIGRANTS

Italian immigrants were victimized so frequently that in 1901 the Society for the Protection of Italian immigrants was organized by American philanthropists and Italian Americans. Operating with money from the Italian government and with contributions from people in New York, the society watched over Italians arriving in Boston and New York and those returning to Italy. The society performed many needed services, such as providing room and board at moderate prices for arriving immigrants and helping new arrivals find relatives and friends. It placed immigrants in jobs and formed schools to teach them English and the essentials of American citizenship. The society watched out for the immigrants in America. This included issuing warnings to unregulated banks, which would often make a practice of skimming funds intended for relatives back home, and singling out the scalpers who sold fraudulent steamship tickets to immigrants who hoped to bring their relatives to America. The society was a critical bridge between both lands.[24]

In Boston, the Italian Immigrant Aid Society was subsidized by the Italian government and charged to "protect the Italian against exploitation and to provide for the return to Italy of those who are sick or discouraged."[25]

In addition, because of its arrangement with the Italian government, the society had the "exclusive privilege of recommending Italian immigrants who wished to return to Italy to obtain nominal tickets issued through contract between steamship companies and the government."[26] While the society's sole source of income was a subsidy provided by the Commissariato dell'Emigrazione, it was supervised by the Archdiocese of Boston.

"The Guide to the United States for the Italian Immigrant"

To assist the Italian immigrant en route to America, the Daughters of the American Revolution prepared "The Guide to the United States for the Immigrant Italian,"[27] which provided useful information to the immigrant in a friendly and informative tone. The guide addressed what to consider when entering the country, what to be aware of, what to be concerned about, what the rules were, what the laws were and where opportunities lay.

The guide explained U.S. currency, weights and measurements and let the immigrant know that the immigrant was obliged to undergo a strict examination by various officials and doctors to ascertain whether his coming was in accordance with the provisions of the laws. If the immigrant did not know English and knew nothing about the American laws, the guide suggested he ask for assistance from the agents of the Society for Italian Immigration, which gave free assistance on arrival at Ellis Island:

> *Pin the green card on your coat so they will find you. Immigrants admitted who do not have relatives or friends here are taken by the agents to the office*

of the Society for Italian Immigrants, where they will receive all information and will be accompanied, along with their baggage, either to their respective destinations in other parts of the city or to the railway stations. The Society for Italian Immigrants fixes a small sum as compensation for accompanying the immigrant and for transporting his baggage.

No one is allowed to enter the United States who has been induced or invited to emigrate by promises or offers of work or who has made a contract—verbal or written, implicit or explicit, by which he has been guaranteed work of any kind. Medically and mentally unsound people will be deported.

Be wary of men with badges in railway stations who offer to carry your luggage. They are not officials of the railway company. They are seeking to charge you.

If you need directions, ask the police. At every railway station in New York there are agents of the Society for Italian immigrants. Ask for them as soon as you arrive.

Learn English: All children must go to school until age 14. There is no charge. High schools are free. There are many night schools. The library is free.

Think about working in the country, not the city. Land is cheap. Buy land and farms. There are abandoned farms that can be bought very cheaply. The government has valuable land it sells at a low price in the west. Purchase is typically $500.00. You can also rent land or farms.

You should become a US citizen because 1) it is your first duty of gratitude to the land that has welcomed you, that gives you and your family a prosperous living, the protection of its laws, educates your children and grants you all the privileges that belong to its native sons; 2) It is a duty to yourself and to your family to become a citizen and a voter, to choose the men who are to represent you, who govern you and to see that your rights are respected; 3) A man counts for nothing in the US until he becomes a voter; 4) citizens enjoy exclusive rights and privileges. You will be eligible for certain government positions which a citizen can obtain by passing rather elementary examinations. You could be elected to any office except president; 5) When you become a citizen, your wife also becomes a citizen; 6) if you travel abroad as a citizen you will have the protection of the US government against illegal activities and unjust penalties; 7) As a citizen you will have greater right to public assistance for yourself and family in case of necessity; 8) In the case of accident or death through the negligence of others, there is a right in every state of recovery of earnings through the courts by the wife and children. In some states this right is not granted to the families of those who are not citizens unless they reside in the US.

The guide told how to become a U.S. citizen and gave an overview of U.S. laws:

You cannot carry a concealed weapon (metal knuckles, sand club, dagger, knife, pistol, firearm etc.).

Pistols and firearms must have written licenses. It is a crime to blackmail. All gambling is prohibited. Lotteries are illegal. It is a crime to desecrate the flag. You must have a license to be a peddler.

You cannot have sex with a girl who is not your wife if she is under 18 years of age. (It does not matter if she consents, is of bad character, or if you believe she is older than age 18.)

It is a crime to commit nuisance in the street, a crime to use profane or obscene language, a crime to strike your wife. Bigamy is a crime even if your wife lives in Italy. It is a crime to procure a false certificate of naturalization to vote, a crime to be cruel to animals, a crime to make any improper use of a train ticket, a crime to spit on the sidewalk, floor of any elevated line, floor of any public building such as halls, churches or markets or on the floor of a street car or ferry boat, a crime to beat a mat, carpet or garment in a manner that moves dust onto the streets or occupied spaces, a crime to throw waste paper and sweepings into the street, a crime to throw garbage or any waste out of the window within city limits, a crime to encumber a fire escape, shoot wild birds at any time, to hunt doves or robins or to kill anything in a public park at any time.

In terms of laws about children: it is a crime to ask for anyone to peddle, ask alms, pick rags etc. in the company of a child. Deserting a child under age 6 is a felony. It is a crime for a man to abandon his family, leaving children under 16 years of age unprovided for, or to neglect to provide for them. The court has the right to take away children from parents who have treated them cruelly or abandoned them.

Children ages six to 14 years of age are required to attend school from October 1 to June 1. Children between 14 and 16 who are not at work must attend. Boys 14 to 16 who are at work and have not finished the elementary public-school course must go to night school not less than six hours a week for not less than six weeks a year.

Under US Child Labor Law, no one can employ a child under age 14 while school is in session. No child 14 to 16 shall be employed unless an employment certificate shall have been filed in the office of employment at the place where the child is to work.

No one under age 16 may work more than 9 hours in any day. None one under age 18 may work more than 10 hours in any day. No one under age 18 may operate a rapid elevator. Except on Saturdays and between December 15 and January 1st no girl between 16 and 21 may work in a store more than 10 hours a day. No boy under 18 and no woman under 21 is allowed to clean machinery while it is in motion. No child may work in the basement of any store without the permission of the Board of Health.

Under Newspaper Boy law, no boy under age 10 may sell papers. Boys 10 to 14 may sell till 10 pm. No girl who is under age 16 can sell papers at any time. No boy under 14 may sell papers unless he has a permit and a badge given to him by the District Superintendent of the Board of Education.

Prohibited employment of children. There is a penalty on anyone who employs a child begging, in gathering or picking rags, collecting cigar stumps, bones, or refuse from a market, or in any peddling or wandering occupation. A child cannot be trained for exhibition as rope walker, acrobat, wrestler, contortionist, horseback or bicycle rider. It is against the law to exhibit an insane, idiotic or deformed child, a crime to sell tobacco to anyone under age 16 and to sell liquor to a minor.

Accidents happen. Be careful. A court may award damages if an employer is negligent.

Sundays must be observed. No alcoholic beverages can be sold unless sold as part of a meal. All contracts made on Sunday are void except those of charity and necessity. Legal documents (except wills) executed on Sundays are void. Promissory notes executed on a Sunday are void.

Marriage licenses are required in most states. Birth and death certificates must be issued.

It is important to care for your health. Keep very clean, eat well, sleep in well-ventilated rooms and live as much as possible in the open air. It is never dangerous to sleep with your windows open. If there are mosquitoes, use a net. Avoid bad air, bad food, bad water, bad habits.[28]

Rules of health: Clean water, clean food, clean bodies, clean clothes, clean houses, clean streets keep us healthy. Keep your hands clean and cut your fingernails. Avoid strong drinks. Strong drinks make weak men.

Drink a great deal of water each day. Never give beer or wine to children. Bathe the whole body every day. Bathing prolongs life.

Buy only fresh meat and fresh fish. Do not buy bread and cake at dirty bakeries. Buy clean milk. (Tuberculosis kills five million people a year and spreads through infected milk.) Cover your food and wash all fruits and vegetables. Sweep and dust.

The Board of Health has great power. It can oblige people to keep their homes and living rooms in habitable condition. It has the power to force employers to keep shops and factories in sanitary condition. It takes care of sick children in school.

Beware of medical institutes that advertise in Italian papers, which pretend to cure every kind of disease, even those that are incurable. When sick, go to an American hospital or dispensary.

Use savings banks. It is dangerous to carry money in your pocket or leave it at home, and dangerous to put it in a private bank. Use Savings bonds. There are only four safe ways to send money out of this country: 1) Postal money orders 2) Bank of Naples (a public banking institution heavily capitalized), 3) American Express or 4) almost any national bank or savings bank.

Those who are naturalized American citizens and wish to go to Italy should request a US passport. Italian citizens and those who wish to use an Italian passport should go to the Italian consulate in that city. There are diplomatic and consul offices in Massachusetts in Boston, Lawrence, and Springfield.

Beware of swindling express men, cab men, guides, agents of steamships and hotels, solicitors, porters, men who say they are journalists or lawyers.

Beware of notaries. They are not allowed to draft documents.

Beware of people whose friendship is too easy to make.

Girls and young women should be aware of strange men who offer them well paid positions or who propose marriage.

Be careful in making and accepting change until you know good money from counterfeit and until you can count American money easily.

Do not buy land by lots; do not accept a lot as a gift. Things are given away only when they have no value.

Do not invest in speculative investments; put your money in a savings bank.

Join American clubs, read American papers, and try to adapt yourself to the manners and customs and habits of the American people.

Have your name placed on the roll of the league or union of your trade. Give up all prejudices and remember that all workmen are brothers. It matters not in what province of Italy or nation in the world they were born.

Treat women and children kindly.

Be willing to give evidence in court. Italians are too willing to have recourse to violence in quarrels. The use of brute force is barbarous.

Throw away all the weapons you have.
Speak in a low voice.
Try not to gesticulate and do not get excited in your discussions.
Be particular about your appearance. Dress well and eat better.

Immigration Restriction and Literacy Tests

In America, there was bubbling up a powerful movement to restrict immigration. The key target was the illiterate, unskilled immigrants from southern Italy. There was fear of the unknown and fear that those who lived in America would be outnumbered by the influx of immigrants (and if the immigrants became citizens, outvoted) by those coming to America who did not yet understand what it meant to be an American.

In 1891, Massachusetts senator Henry Cabot Lodge wrote that the immigration into the United States from 1874 to 1889 amounted to 6,418,633 persons without counting the 1884 overland immigration from Canada or Mexico.

"To put it in another form," he wrote, "the immigration into the United States during the last 16 years is equal to one-tenth of the entire population of the country at the present time, and has furnished probably every four years enough votes to decide a presidential election, if properly distributed. It is apparent that immigration is increasing in quantity and the next point is to determine its quality. The emigration from Italy comes largely from the southern provinces—Naples and Sicily. A much smaller population is being drawn from the finer population of northern Italy."[29]

He quoted a Mr. Alden, general-counsel in Rome, saying in 1866:

> *As to the habits and morals of the emigrants to the United States from the northern and central portions of Italy, both men and women are sober and industrious and as rule trustworthy and moral. They are generally strong, powerful workers and capable of enduring great fatigue. A less favorable view may be taken of the emigrants from the southern districts and Sicily. These are the most illiterate parts of Italy and in these districts, brigandage was for many years extremely prevalent.*[30]

"While it is apparent that immigration is increasing," Lodge continued, "it is showing at the same time a marked tendency to deteriorate in character."[31]

He argued for restrictions on immigration and proposed new immigration laws that would require immigrants to bring from their native country—from the U.S. consul or other diplomatic representative—an effective certificate that they are not offending any existing laws of the United Sates. He argued further that the test should require a medical certificate to exclude unsound and diseased persons. He also issued a strong battle cry against allowing illiterate immigrants into the country. "It is a truism to say that one of the greatest dangers to our free government is ignorance," Lodge stated.

We spend millions annually in educating our children that they may become fit to be citizens and rulers of the Republic. We are ready to educate the children who come to us from other countries. But it is not right to ask us to take in annually a large body of persons who are totally illiterate and who are, for the most part, beyond the age at which education can be imparted. We have the right to exclude illiterate persons from our immigration and this test, combined with the others of a more general character, would in all probability shut out a large portion of the present immigrants. It would reduce in a discriminatory manner the total number of immigrants and thereby greatly benefit the labor market and help to maintain the role of American wages. At the same time, it would sift the immigrants who come to this country and would shut out in very large measure those elements which tend to lower the quality of American citizenship and which now in many cases gather in dangerous masses in the slums of our great cities. The measure proposed would benefit every honest immigrant who really desired to come to the United States and become an American citizen. It would exclude many, if not all, of the persons whose presence no one desires and whose exclusion is demanded by our duty to our own citizens and to American institutions. Above all, it would be a protection and help to our workingmen, who are more directly interested in this question than anyone else can possibly be.[32]

Senator Lodge was not the only one on this bandwagon. When discussing the "masses of peasantry" from Italy, Hungary, Austria and Russia in the 1890s, MIT president Francis Walker expressed the combination of dismay, disdain and pessimism that characterized New England's Anglo-Saxon mind: "These people have not history behind them which is of a nature to give encouragement. They have none of the inherited instincts and tendencies which make it comparatively easy to deal with the immigration of olden times. They are beaten men from beaten races; representing the worst failures in the struggle for existence. Centuries are against them as centuries were on the side of those who formerly came to the United States."[33]

THE IMMIGRATION RESTRICTION LEAGUE (IRL)

In 1894, twenty-five-year-old Prescott Farnsworth Hall formed the Immigration Restriction League (IRL) in Boston with his close friends Charles Warren and Robert DeCourcy Ward. All were members of the Harvard class of 1889. They formed IRL out of fear that the American democracy, founded by Anglo-Saxon settlers using Anglo-Saxon law and government, could perish under the avalanche of exotic immigrants.[34]

The IRL raised specific questions, such as: Was America great because of the hard work of successive waves of immigrants coming to the nation's shores looking for opportunity? Or was American greatness a by-product of its Anglo-Saxon settlers?

In 1899, the governor of New York, Theodore Roosevelt, warned, "If we stand idly by, if we seek merely swollen, slothful ease and ignoble peace, if we shrink from the hard contests where men must win at hazard of their lives and at the risk of all they hold dear, then the bolder and stronger peoples will pass us by, and will win for themselves the domination of the world."[35]

These words were a warning to Anglo-Saxons who risked being overtaken by the more vigorous immigrant groups: "New England of the future will belong to the descendants of the immigrants of yesterday and today because the descendants of the Puritans have lacked the courage to live."[36]

The IRL had an elite approach and worked closely with Henry Cabot Lodge, who had moved over to the U.S. Senate by 1893 and would take over as chair of its immigration committee.

Immigration regulation, rather than an aberration, was part of a national movement that turned its back on the laissez-faire philosophy of government and sought to transform American society and control the social changes roiling the country in the late 1800s.

Two patrician members of the IRL were known for their support of other Progressive reforms: Joseph Lee, "father of American playgrounds," and Robert Woods, a leader in Boston's settlement house movement.[37]

Early advocacy was free of ethnic prejudice, yet they were unhappy with the current immigration laws. Even with the opening of Ellis Island

and expansion of excludable categories, the IRL thought the quality of immigrants was deteriorating.[38]

The IRL proposed increasing the head tax from one dollar per immigrant to at least ten dollars and possibly as high as fifty dollars, requiring a consular certificate for each immigrant acknowledging their character and desirability and a mandate that every immigrant had to read and write in his or her own language. The IRL, however, thought an education test in English would be unfair.

The three founders of the IRL were allowed to visit Ellis Island on at least three occasions between 1895 and 1896. In April 1895, Hall visited Ellis Island and deemed its operation greatly improved over prior years, although he saw too many illiterate, unskilled workers, especially Italian, during the visit. Hall told the *Boston Herald*: "As nearly as I could judge in the case of the Italians whom I saw at Ellis Island there was in general a close connection between illiteracy and a general undesirability."[39]

In 1896, members of the IRL examined 3,174 Italian immigrants and found 58 percent were illiterate. Yet to their dismay, only 197 were excluded from entry. In just a few days, Ellis Island officials had let in almost 2,000 illiterate Italians. IRL found only 4.5 percent of the immigrants from northwestern Europe coming through Ellis Island were illiterate, while 48 percent of those from southern and eastern Europe could not read.

Senator Henry Cabot Lodge and the IRL

Senator Lodge used the research done by the IRL in his continued proposals for restricted immigration and a literacy test. In a speech in the Senate on March 16, 1896, Senator Lodge argued,

Immigration has two sides—economic and social. On the economic side there is no one thing which does so much to bring about a reduction of wages and injure the American wage earner as the unlimited introduction of cheap foreign labor through unrestricted immigration. If we have any regard for the welfare, the wages, or the standard of living of American working men, we should take immediate steps to restrict foreign immigration. There is no present danger at all levels to our working men from the coming of skilled mechanics or trained and educated men with a settled occupation, for immigrants of this class will never seek to lower the American standard of life and wages; on the contrary they desire the same standard for themselves. But there is an appalling danger to the American wage earner from the flood of low, unskilled, ignorant, foreign labor, which has poured into the country for some years past but accepts a standard of living so low that American working men cannot compete with it. The danger this immigration threatens

Henry Cabot Lodge. *Boston Public Library*.

to the quality of citizenship is far worse. That danger is changing the quality of our race and citizenship through the infusion of races whose traditions, inheritances, thoughts, and beliefs are totally alien to ours and with whom we have never assimilated and have never been associated in the past. The danger has begun. The time has come, if not to stop, at least to check, to sift and restrict those immigrants. In careless strength, with a generous hand, we have kept our gates wide open to all the world. If we do not close them, we should at least place sentinels beside them to challenge those who would pass through. The gates which admit men to the United States and to citizenship in the great republic should no longer be left unguarded.[40]

Establishment of Bureau of Immigration and Naturalization

In 1906, Congress established the Bureau of Immigration and Naturalization. Department of Justice officers were in charge of examining the petitions for citizenship filed in court. The bureau was split into two divisions: the Division of Immigration and the Division of Naturalization. The Immigration Division handled arrivals into the country and general immigration matters. Naturalization was charged with all matters relating to granting citizenship to aliens. Judges kept their independence and continued to rule on naturalization petitions. The findings and recommendations of the newly formed bureau formed the basis for the court's determination as to whether a petitioner's request would be admitted, denied or require future investigation. This change to central executive branch control over the examination process was fundamental.[41]

The information petitioners were required to file exploded. They had to provide precise life history data: time and date of birth of the applicant, wife and children, place and date of marriage, date and port of embarkation, port of entry, information on period between immigration and naturalization, name of vessel on which they arrived, information about occupants, information about amount of time spent continuously in United States, the state in which they sought citizenship and their hometown, province or region in Europe.[42]

The Citizenship Process

To become citizens, they had to be in the country at least two years before filing a Declaration of Citizenship and five years to file an official Petition for Citizenship (Naturalization Petition). Information was often different between these two documents, especially if the address or occupation changed. Copies of the declarations were attached to the petition. In October 1911, copies of certificates of arrival were included. These certificates detailed when an immigrant arrived in America, at what port and on what vessel.

The Lodge Bill and Literacy Tests

Senator Lodge's communications, writings, thoughts and speeches led to what is known as the Lodge Bill, which would have barred illiterate immigrants over the age of sixteen. The literacy test would consist of twenty-five words from the U.S. Constitution translated into the immigrant's native language. The bill was overwhelmingly approved by the Senate (52–10) and the House (217–36). Since 50 percent of all illiterate immigrants entering the United States were Italian, the Lodge Bill was perceived to have an anti-Italian bias. Senator Lodge denied this. However, both New York commissioner of immigration Joseph Senner and Herman Stump, the head of the Immigration Bureau, urged President Grover Cleveland to veto the idea.[43]

Stump argued that any laws should "be tempered with sympathy for our unfortunate fellow beings who are so compelled by adversity to abandon their homes to seek asylum in an unknown country." He said America needed unskilled labor to "construct railroads, macadamize our highways, build sewers, and clear lands, thereby freeing up native-born Americans from jobs they found distasteful and allowing them to engage in the higher and more remunerative trades and occupations."[44]

These arguments swayed Cleveland, who vetoed the literacy bill. Congress was unable to override it.

President Cleveland stated: "It is said, however, that the quality of recent immigration is undesirable. The time is quite within recent memory when the same thing was said of immigrants who, with their descendants, are now numbered among our best citizens."[45]

Cleveland continued, asserting that he would "rather admit a thousand immigrants who, though unable to read or write, seek among us only a home and opportunity to work, than to admit one of those unruly agitators and enemies of governmental control, who can not only read and write but delights in arousing by inflammatory speech the illiterate and peaceful to discontent and tumult."[46]

The Dillingham Commission Report

The 1910 United States Senate Report of the Immigration Commission is more commonly known as the "Dillingham Commission Report," named after the U.S. senator from Vermont who recommended the study. It has forty-two volumes. Senator Henry Cabot Lodge served on the Dillingham Commission, which reported that southern Italians ranked among the lowest in literacy rates of foreign-born persons from 1899 to 1910. Only about 55 percent of southern Italians could read or write in their native language, compared to 97 to 98 percent of Germans, for example. The Dillingham Commission began to study the problem of 1910 immigration. Dillingham was a restrictionist. The report to Congress, which claimed to be scientific and objective, announced that since 1880, the character of immigration had undergone a fundamental change for the worse. It classified all immigrant classes by race, implying old-stock Anglo-Saxon Americans were basically superior and the newcomers, such as the Italians, were generally inferior, prone to crime and eventually became paupers and burdens to society. The commission favored restrictions on immigration and recommended the literacy test.

The Italian government, Italian newspapers and societies in the United States all opposed it. Italians at that time had no political muscle. Official government reports also stereotyped northern and southern Italians. The Dillingham Commission reported that

> *Northern Italians are held in higher estimation by the natives than Italians from the Southern part of Italy....The Southern Italians are slow in becoming Americanized. They live in colonies, have very little association with natives, are suspicious of Americans, do not trust their money to the banks, and trade at American shops as little as possible. While industrious, they are said to be impulsive, erratic, and quick to leave their jobs if they see*

apparent advantage elsewhere. It seems generally agreed that the Sicilians are less steady and less inclined to stick to a job day in and day out than other races.[47]

In Boston, the Dillingham Commission reported, where Italian families took in more boarders than any other city, southern Italians earned an average of $338 a year and 29 percent earned less than $200. Yet when family income as a whole was taken into account, southern Italians earned an average of $534, greater than any immigrant group other than the Irish.

Of all the large Boston ethnic groups surveyed by the Dillingham Commission, the statistics showed that the South Italians from the North End neighborhood far and away were leaders in the category called "population stability." Of the more than three hundred families surveyed, the largest number of any ethnic group in the Boston study, more than 74 percent had resided in the same neighborhood for the entire time they had been in the United States. Southern Italians led the large immigrant groups for "neighborhood continuity" regardless of the amount of time they spent in America. For example, for people in the United States less than five years, 84 percent of southern Italians had spent their whole lives in the North End neighborhood.[48]

Literacy requirements were again introduced in 1912, and though passed by the Congress, the legislation was vetoed by President William Taft. In 1915, another literacy bill passed, and President Woodrow Wilson vetoed it because he felt literacy tests denied equal opportunity to those who were not educated. On February 15, 1917, the Immigration Act of 1917 was passed by the Sixty-Fourth Congress with an overwhelming majority overriding President Wilson's veto. This law affected European immigration with a provision barring all immigrants over age sixteen who were illiterate. Literacy was defined as the ability to read thirty to forty words in their own language from an ordinary text. (The law was subsequently modified in 1924 and 1952.)[49]

IMMIGRATING THE "RIGHT WAY"

It is interesting to note that today in discussions of immigration, many people say they want immigrants to enter legally—"the right way"— as their ancestors did. This point of view does not take into account that

Anna of Etna Pastry. *Vito Aluia collection.*

the U.S. immigration system now is very different from the immigration system of the early twentieth century. When many families arrived in the United States, there were no numerical limitations on immigration, no requirement to have an existing family or employment relationship with someone in the country and no requirement to obtain a visa prior to arriving. The definition of who is "legal" and who is not changes with the evolving immigration laws.

In some cases, claiming that a family came "legally" is simply inaccurate. Unauthorized immigration has been a reality for generations. Between 1925 and 1965, 200,000 unauthorized Europeans legalized their status through the Registry Act, through "pre-examination"—a process that allowed them to leave the United States voluntarily and reenter legally with a visa (a "touch back" program)—or through discretionary rules that allowed immigration officials to suspend deportations in "meritorious cases."

In the 1940s and 1950s, several thousand deportations a year were suspended; approximately 73 percent of those who benefited were Europeans (mostly Germans and Italians).[50]

POST–WORLD WAR II IMMIGRATION

Time marched on. Post–World War II immigration to the North End was markedly different than before. Italians living south of Rome who wished to emigrate had many more options. Italians were courted by a number of countries, including Australia. Between 1945 and 1983, some 400,000 Italians, usually unskilled and with limited education, moved to Australia. Moving to northern Italy (which significantly improved economically in the 1950s and 1960s) was easier culturally and financially than moving overseas.

EXODUS TO THE SUBURBS

In the 1980s and 1990s, many Italians moved out of the North End to the suburbs. Immigration from Italy was significantly reduced. By the 2000 census, Italian Americans were a minority in the North End for the first time since 1920.[51]

For the most part, as the generations evolved, the Italian Americans in the North End assimilated into the American culture. The North End became gentrified. Its Italian immigrant roots were a significant part of its economic success. The gentrification of the North End and its thriving economy depended on marketing it as an Italian neighborhood—even as James Pasto points out, paradoxically, gentrification had resulted in the diminution of the Italian American residents. Italian restaurants, cafés, bakeries and pastry shops have flourished due to the neighborhood's wealthier residential clientele as well as the influx of visitors and tourists who came to experience Boston's Puritan and Revolutionary center *and* its "Little Italy."[52]

3

THE NORTH END

When the southern Italians (those from Avellino, Calabria, Abruzzi and Sicily) arrived in the United States from Italy, they faced a new culture, a new language and new challenges. Leaving their Italian villages and arriving at Ellis Island and seeing the hustle and bustle of a big city, tall skyscrapers and elevated trains must have been a startling experience. There must have been both fear and excitement. Opportunities and danger were around the corner.

It is not surprising that those who then came to Boston gravitated toward the North End—an enclave of people from southern Italy who were similar to them. It felt familiar and bonded them together with their common connections to families, friends and the villages they left behind.[53]

CHAIN MIGRATION

Chain migration led to the growth of an Italian enclave. Men would come first and then bring over wives and children, encouraging others from the village to come too. Once the Italians established homes, they would send for relatives and friends, who became boarders in the houses of the original immigrants. The boarders eventually found their own homes and repeated the process. Chain migration was stronger in the North End than in other American Italian communities.[54]

LIFE IN THE ENCLAVE

Living in the enclave allowed the mostly southern Italians to adjust slowly to the new country. This was a strength in helping them cope, but it was also a negative because it slowed down their assimilation into America. It also slowed down their learning English. Remaining illiterate and not speaking English limited the jobs available to the new immigrants. Many of the men who arrived could not even read a steamship ticket in their native Italian. Only those with exceptional energy were able to return home from a ten-hour day of ditch digging or plastering and sit down with a grammar book to learn English. This kept most tied to the enclave, where at least they could be understood and communicate.[55]

A study of the marriage records in the North End churches illustrates the significance of Italian provincial loyalties. Italians in Boston

North End of Boston. *Boston Public Library.*

Children playing, Stillman Street, 1923. *City of Boston Archives.*

consistently preferred marriage with individuals from their own province or region, frequently marrying individuals from a place as close to their village as possible.[56]

In the enclave, as in the villages in Italy they left, family mattered most. La *famiglia* was nominally a patriarchal system. The father, as the head of the family, was responsible for arbitrating all family disputes and making all decisions that had a relationship between his family and the outside world. He worked hard and kept his family out of poverty. The father was deeply respected in the Italian family. The mother managed all internal affairs of the family, was keeper of the hearth, managed the finances and arranged the marriages of her children. In a world in which the family status was judged not by the occupation of the father but by the signs of well-being that emanated from the household, the mother played an important role in maintaining that status. *La via veccia* (the old way) became the value system. To the southern Italian, a well-educated person was one who was properly schooled in what the family considered proper conduct. Hard physical labor was positive because it prepared a son for the family responsibilities

Children playing,
Stillman Street, 1923.
*Boston Landmarks
Commission.*

of manhood and a daughter for her role as a woman within the family unit. The greatest offense of all was disrespect for the family.[57]

NORTH END: FIRST SLUM NEIGHBORHOOD

By 1850, the North End had become Boston's first slum neighborhood. When the Italians arrived in the North End, they lived in tenements. In 1896, the Boston City Council described the tenements on Fleet Street:

> *In none of the houses is there any ventilation. Air shafts were not thought of when those houses were built. Though the sun shines in some rooms, all the lower rooms are very dark. From cellar to roof, each house is very dirty and battered. In many rooms pieces of the ceiling have fallen in and more is ready to fall. The wooden houses on both sides of the alley shake so much as one walks about them and their floors are so far from level, it is surprising they have not collapsed, in spite of the support being given them by adjoining buildings.[58]*

North End housing consisted of small apartments in four- to five-story tenements. Families often lived in two or three rooms with cold water plumbing in the basement. There were no elevators. It took stamina to walk up five flights after a long day of work. The men who lived in the tenements had no money and needed work. Ten or twelve men would

Teaching infant care to Italian immigrant mothers at the welfare clinic at the North End Union, 1920. *(North End Union)*

Left: Teaching Italian immigrant mothers, 1920. *North End Union.*

Below: Webster Court street sweepers, 1909. *Boston Athenaeum.*

rent one room. Each paid $0.25 to $0.30 a week and was entitled to a fire for cold winter days. In 1872, fire destroyed eight hundred buildings in Boston's sixty-five-acre business district adjacent to the North End, causing $80 million in losses and creating twenty-five thousand unemployed, most of them North Enders.[59]

In 1895, 1.5 percent of the city of Boston's population was Italian; by 1902, more than 60 percent of the population was Italian. Very little English was spoken. Most newspapers and other publications were in Italian. In 1902, more than 19 percent of the real estate in the North End was owned by Italian residents.

Hanover Street, 1909.
Library of Congress.

The congested quarters and lack of proper sanitation took their toll. In 1898 and 1899, the North End had the largest total number of deaths in the city from pneumonia, meningitis, typhoid fever and diphtheria. The North End had the second-largest number of deaths from infant cholera and bronchitis. Home to the poorest immigrants, the North End was the most crowded one hundred acres of land on earth in 1900.[60]

The North End was small. As Stephen Puleo noted, "It was 100 acres and roughly the same size as parking lots at Disney World."[61] Its size created a sense of stability. Although the neighborhood had its hardships with congestion and disease, in a positive way it helped Italian immigrants bridge the gap from perceiving themselves as residents of a distant regional enclave to viewing themselves as residents of an Italian community.[62]

NORTH END BEFORE THE ITALIANS

It is interesting to note that the North End did not start off as an Italian neighborhood. Before the American Revolutionary War, it had some of the most impressive residences in North America. At one time, the North End was home to many of the wealthiest merchants. The end of the war brought a demographic shift. The affluent Loyalists left the North End for the more prestigious Beacon Hill because as the city grew, the North End was too close to the docks and the commercial part of Boston. By 1800, many North End mansions were vacant, and German and Irish families moved in. Sanitation did not exist. The neighborhood became predominantly Irish and Jewish, until the Italians moved in. In 1876, fewer than one thousand Italians lived in the North End (representing only 4 percent of the area's population.) In 1900, there were twenty-four thousand Italians (representing 62 percent of the population), and in 1920, there were forty thousand Italians living in the North End (representing 97 percent of the population). By the time the Italians arrived, the neighborhood had long been identified as undesirable by upper- and middle-class Americans.[63]

In the early days of immigration, the waterfront was like the Bowery in New York, with dance halls and bistros for the seamen who came in on the boats that landed at the waterfront. The New York boat at Rowes Wharf sailed every evening at five o'clock, the Eastern Steamship went to Nova Scotia, the Merchant line went to Baltimore and United Fruit (then called the Great White Fleet) hauled bananas in from Central America.[64] The North End teemed with industry and grittiness.

The Importance of Geography

The reason that the wealthier Bostonians left the North End (proximity to the docks and the commercial section of Boston) was a major reason the illiterate and uneducated Italian immigrants found opportunity there. The North End was geographically unique because of its proximity to both the downtown section and the dock and port area. This afforded the North End Italians access within walking distance to a multitude of jobs. Those who walked downtown could work as laborers, fruit vendors, barbers, waiters and porters in the downtown hotels. The Boston subway system was in the midst of construction. The Park Street Station (a major hub) opened in 1897. Construction on the subway system provided ample jobs for unskilled

North Square and Paul Revere House, 1900. *Vito Aluia collection.*

Italian boys at fishing wharf. *Lewis Wickes Hines National Child Labor Collection, Library of Congress.*

Italian laborers as well as skilled craftsmen. At the same time, the port of Boston was becoming one of the most active ports on the Eastern Seaboard, providing jobs for immigrants as warehousemen, longshoremen, shippers, merchants and packers.[65]

The geographic proximity to downtown afforded the Italian immigrant a convenient opportunity to observe and eventually become part of the American mainstream. Hundreds of residents walked from the North End to downtown daily to work. This exposure to non-Italians (although difficult because of the discrimination the Italians faced) aided the confidence and assimilation process of the North End Italians.

Italians could walk to a downtown job, get a bigger American picture during the day and then walk home to the familiar enclave at night.

NORTH END EMPLOYMENT

In 1909, the dominant industry for Italian immigrant men was construction. Construction was ideal because of the nature of the work and because they did not need to know how to speak English. The same dialect could be used by all workers in the beginning, and family well-being was enhanced as more members of the family joined the business in subsequent years.[66]

As North Ender Joseph Tassinari put it, "They went everywhere for jobs, one week or month in Maine, then Connecticut or down the Cape. They went wherever there was work. It was a hard life but they had to do it for their families. This was common among the North End workers."[67]

Second to construction was working as a barber. Before 1905, barber licenses were not required in Massachusetts. After that, a candidate had to apprentice under a licensed barber. Steady business, regular hours, limited restrictions and a respectable income made working as a barber a good profession for the Italian man.[68]

Fruit peddlers and vendors were also professions immigrant Italian men chose. Many Sicilians also became fishermen and bakers.[69]

The two greatest employers of women were as confectionary workers and as tailors/seamstresses. Candy companies were ideal for women, as working there did not require any special skill or training. Many of the women were illiterate. Women started off boxing chocolates, and hard workers progressed to candy dipping.[70]

The greatest number of women in the North End, however, did not work outside of the home. They were homemakers.[71]

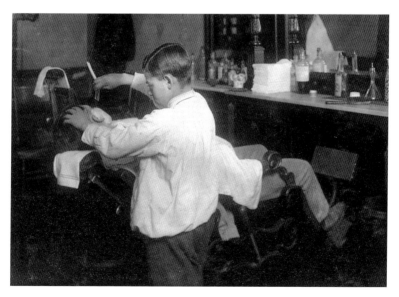

Twelve-year-old Frank DeNatale working at his father's barbershop, 1917. *Lewis Wickes Hines National Child Labor Collection, Library of Congress.*

SETTLEMENT IN THE NORTH END AND THE IMPORTANCE OF THE NORTH BENNET SCHOOL

Sociologist Robert Woods noted conditions in the North End represented "the waste of ability and genius."[72] Two women, Harriet Clark Caswell and Pauline Agassiz Shaw,[73] understood this and took actions that had a profound effect on the North End. They had a settlement perspective, not a philanthropic one. The settlement perspective is that even well-intentioned charity merely creates a need for more charity because it never addresses the underlying causes of poverty. It only tides the poor over for another year of minimal subsistence. Putting a coal chute in a building keeps it warm, for example, but it does not address the underlying energy efficiency of the

Top: Boschetto Bakery, 1917. *Vito Aluia collection.*

Bottom: Hancock School evening embroidery class, 1920. *North End Union.*

building. Charity supports the status quo. In comparison, an action, such as building a pedestrian bridge, permits people of multiple classes to gain sight and perspectives beyond the status quo.[74]

In the late 1800s, the North End presented many opportunities for improvement. Harriet Clark Caswell formed the North End Industrial Home in 1880. She started with $500 and noticed how many North Enders lacked winter clothing. She did not buy them clothing; instead, she went down the street and invited women to learn how to mend garments for themselves. In just a few weeks, enrollees in her class numbered two hundred.

Caswell did not stop there. She found a location on Salem Street, and there she taught women how to sew and use sewing machines and provided

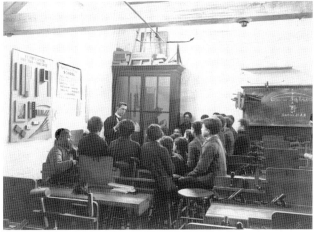

Top: North Bennet School instruction, 1892. *Boston Public Library.*

Bottom: Hancock School evening millinery class, 1892. *Boston Public Library.*

North Bennet School sewing class, 1934. *Boston Public Library.*

an opportunity to purchase sewing machines at a lower rate, launching home-based businesses. She started a laundry room in the basement and provided instructions on laundering as an opportunity for income. Renting laundry tubs or using their own laundry equipment, women began starting their own businesses. Caswell also started scrubbing services, training women for employment cleaning railroad cars, business offices and public buildings.

In 1881, Caswell leased an entire building at 39 North Bennet Street with an option to purchase and started the North End Industrial Home, focusing on the needs of the young children, girls and women of the North End. The lease was financed by Pauline Agassiz Shaw and King's Chapel in Boston. There Caswell taught women laundering and scrubbing, sewing and carpentry and provided a library, amusement room, day nursery and kindergarten. She organized a carpentry shop for boys and established ground rules. She told the boys in the class they must make every movement of their tools *tell* in some way (tell meaning to provide a meaningful result), or they could not keep them. She immersed herself in the North End.

In 1885, the North End Industrial Home appealed to the Boston School Committee to allow public students to be trained at NEIH, and boys and girls in the North End began attending NEIH for weekly two-hour sessions. Caswell added programs—clay modeling, dressmaking, military drill, shoe making and repair—to her vocational school. Cooking and carpentry were modified. Sewing, laundering and scrubbing were dropped.

Pauline Agassiz Shaw and friends bought the building and formed a nonprofit, and in 1885 the North Bennet Industrial School was born. In 1886, a fire broke out and the building had to be rebuilt. The mission shifted. The school still believed that the inability to do anything well represented the underlying cause of poverty in the North End but added that the school's chief aim was to give education—the use of *both* manual training *and* intellectual work for educational purposes. Due to poverty, lack of interest, family circumstances or a combination of all these factors, many fourteen-year-old students left school after the sixth grade, which afforded them few prospects other than unskilled labor. The school created a pre-vocational program with three objectives:

Influence boys and girls to stay in school beyond age fourteen;
Build an interest in school through manual and industrial work; and
Assist students with trade selection and preparation.

The school added social services and a reading room. By the late 1880s, it had installed showers and offered weekly baths to boys. By 1910, the school was sponsoring at least eighty-five social activities, including dances, parties and outings.

In 1914, the school asked supporters to donate clothing suitable for young men, reasoning it might keep boys in school longer and improve their career options. In 1920, it envisioned summer camps for North End families—Boxford Camp for young children and families, Caddy Camp for boys and both travel and stay-at-home camps for those who stayed in the North End.

Other social workers also reached out. Some reformers sought to establish and support free employment agencies for immigrants and destroy the padrone labor system of brokers who victimized their fellow countrymen as they arrived in the United States. Others worked to procure the passage of child labor laws and the strict observance of compulsory education legislation.

Italian immigrants gained notoriety (and the wrath of social workers) because their children were seldom permitted to obtain adequate schooling. While complaining that their own lack of education kept them from getting

North End children on a field trip, 1890. *Vito Aluia collection.*

North End mission teaching Italian immigrant girl to read, 1868–1902. *Boston Public Library.*

better jobs, parents nonetheless sent their children to work (rather than school) to supplement the family income. Although in time most Italians complied with the minimum requirements of compulsory education laws, they secured jobs for their children after school hours. When Italian children reached the legal age of fourteen, they were "to an alarmingly high degree" withdrawn from school and put to work. Despite dire predictions that Italians were in a "cycle of poverty," by 1900 they had begun progressing from unskilled labor into commercial, trade and professional classes, including printing, bricklaying, carpentering, import and export firms, banking, law and medicine. Notwithstanding complaints of reformers and laments of immigration workers, financial success at this time did not require education. Ambition and cunning could, and often did, overcome illiteracy.

The Italians were able to save money due to their willingness to subsist on small amounts. They brought in boarders for additional income and worked hard. Part of what drove them was to send money back to poorer family members who remained in Italy and the desire to purchase a home in America.

North Bennet School was also the site of the first credit union organization in a settlement house. Joseph Campana, known as the "father of credit unions," helped organize the union, which opened on September 1, 1921, with capital of $14.25. When the charter was granted, there were 11 members. Two months later, there were 53 members with combined savings of $1,486. Two years later, 243 members had contributed assets of $50,999. Children were encouraged to contribute pennies and dimes. Loans were given to local people whom no other bank would ever approve of because at that time the

North End was considered a high-risk slum. People worked hard and used their loans to build businesses, repair homes and upgrade neighborhoods. The Social Service Credit Union made most of this possible.[75]

North End Stabilization

The North End stabilized in the years before the outbreak of World War I (1900–1910). It developed into a strong Italian community and became the center of Italian life in Boston. Even those who left the North End came back to shop and socialize.

Yet for decades the North End remained a slum. It was an ethnic enclave with social decline, rundown buildings, dirt, poverty and violence. This reinforced American prejudice against the Italians.

North End: "Street Corner Boys" and "College Boys"

From 1937 to 1938, sociologist William Foote Whyte decided to study the North End and moved in with an Italian family living in the slum. He lived in the North End for three and half years and wrote a book about his experiences. The book was required reading in most colleges and focused on social structure, social mobility and the patterns of racketeering and political corruption.[76] The North End had developed a reputation as a depressed and dangerous part of Boston, dominated by corrupt politicians and racketeers. It was seen as a place in which subversive beliefs, crime and illegal activities were widely diffused. While living there, Whyte observed that within the Italian community there were smaller communities aggregated along local identities. Social lives were organized around such boundaries because people from the same towns settled together, celebrated the patron saints of their villages and created mutual societies. Immigrants from Italy's northern and central regions (those from Rome, Venice, Piedmont and Genoa) who had slightly better educational backgrounds had already improved their economic prospects and looked down on the southern Italians. He observed that the first generation of immigrants relied on family ties and that few of the older immigrants maintained prominent positions in the community. The big shots were racketeers who controlled illegal gambling activities and political bases.[77]

North End alley baseball along clotheslines, 1909. *Vito Aluia collection.*

Whyte found two patterns in the young: "street corner boys" and "college boys." Street corner boys, Whyte noted, were the majority. They had little formal education and spent most of their time in street activities because they did not have steady employment. They belonged to gangs for which the center of social interaction was on street corners in proximity to saloons, barbershops and poolrooms. Each corner group had its own leader who was respected in that group when dealing with racketeers and politicians.

The college boys were fewer in number. Since they attended college, they had opportunities to improve their own social status following professional careers.

Whyte concluded that the problem with the North End was not lack of organization but failure of its own social organization to mesh with the society around it. The slum was not a disorganized place. The real problem, he believed, was that the organization of the Italian community did not fit in with the rest of American society.

In America, the idea of social mobility was valued, as were intelligence, creativity, talent and hard work. The promise of social improvement and material gain in the Italian community was related to careers in politics as racketeers. That was in large part because the U.S. social system strongly discriminated against Italian immigrants and rewarded those who could slough off all their Italian characteristics. The system penalized those who were not fully Americanized. If an Italian American remained loyal to his group and climbed the hierarchal structure of his community to the point of becoming a racketeer or political boss, he would become an outcast of American society. If he succeeded following the opposite path of education, becoming a professional, he would leave his original community to move to a better neighborhood.

The North End Italians' history with politics is significant. They came mainly came from the south of Italy, where they had learned through centuries of conquest and oppression to mistrust all government. They were extremely apathetic about obtaining their citizenship and did not really believe their united voice could be effectively used at the polls. In 1868, only twelve people with Italian surnames voted in Boston, all from the North End. They did not control their own ward. In 1871, this was Ward 2. In 1909, only 20.8 percent of the Italian population surveyed had American citizenship. Irish politicians, representing a minority of the population, were elected every time. In 1915, when it looked like the Italians were beginning to gain political control of the North End, it was combined with the West End and South End wards. The political machine of Martin Lomasney kept Italians out of local politics for another twenty years.[78]

THE IMPACT OF THE WEST END (ABUTTING THE NORTH END)

Sociologist Herbert Gans studied the West End (which abuts the North End) in 1957–58.[79] At that time, 42 percent of the West End households were Italian. Most of them were southern Italians with less formal education and manual occupations. He noted that the West Enders were not frustrated seekers of middle-class values. Their way of life constituted a distinct and independent working-class subculture that bore little resemblance to the middle class. Making money was not considered as important as friendship and family ties. West End Italians ignored one another's incomes. They judged the material well-being of the family by the family's lifestyle. Women's abilities as wives, mothers and housekeepers were very valuable. Marriage outside of the ethnic group was not easily accepted.[80]

Gans found the assimilation process of Italian immigrants into American society was very slow. At the end of the 1950s, immigrants' social relations were still limited to relatives and close friends. Friendships

North Street Grocery. *Vito Aluia Collection.*

Men playing a game. *Anthony Riccio collection.*

Blackstone Grocery
Market, 1940s. *Vito
Aluia collection.*

were usually intra-ethnic because the relationships were created during childhood. He noted that although the children who became the adults of the second generation retained little of the Italian culture, they did retain most of its social structure. The acculturation of Italian immigrants happened quickly. There was a substantial difference between the first and second generations.[81]

SECOND GENERATION OF ITALIANS IN THE NORTH END

In 1950, second-generation immigrants were already grown up. They had lost most of their Italian culture. Second-generation immigrants did not identify with Italy and the towns their parents came from. Only a small group of individuals had preserved a connection to the Italian culture. Some habits survived, such as food traditions. The second-generation Italians were still making their own pasta and cooked Italian dishes for the family. The Italian language survived in the form of local dialects. Generally, first-generation Italian immigrants did not learn English and spoke to their children in Italian.[82]

THIRD GENERATION OF ITALIANS IN THE NORTH END

By the third generation, Italian language and dialects had disappeared. The main structure that played a decisive role in the process of second-generation

North End celebration of V-J Day, 1945. *Vito Aluia collection.*

acculturation to America was the school. The education system intended to "Americanize" immigrant families.[83]

This continued on even after World War II. In 1962, the second generation of Italian American immigrants (sons and daughters of the Italian immigrants who were born and educated in the United States) were determined to establish a different relationship with their cultural heritage and the American culture. During this period, the Italian Americans in the North End began to develop a new perception of their own identity. There was a collective transformation. One of the lowest regarded and most discriminated against ethnic groups modified the perception of its own image and became proud of its cultural heritage and ethnic roots. Part of the reason for this was what was occurring in Italy. The economic development of Italy after World War II in the 1950s and 1960s is known as "the economic miracle." Italy's economic conditions dramatically changed. Fashion and luxury exports to the United States became important. Italy became a popular destination for American tourists. Italy began to be associated with culture, beauty, fashion and style.[84]

In the 1930s, the North End began to change. Encouraged by the ambience of the area and low rents, several artists moved to the area. This was the first time that nonimmigrants had consciously chosen to live there in more than one hundred years. Robert S. Chase, portrait painter and decorator, left a studio on Beacon Hill to restore a beautiful home on Snowhill Street. He later designed the bronzes in Paul Revere Mall.[85]

By the 1930s, the Italian population was decreasing. Sons and daughters got married and moved to the suburbs.

Civic Improvements to the North End and the Rise of Italian Power

Mayor Curley authorized the building of the Prado, known also as the Paul Revere Mall. Several narrow tenement streets were cleared out, and the mall was established in 1933. The land the Prado stands on was originally part of the pasture belonging to Christopher Stanley, who bequeathed some of his land for the establishment of a free school, thus becoming the first private benefactor of public education.[86]

A bronze equestrian statue of Paul Revere originally modeled by Cyrus E. Dallin in 1885 was cast and placed on the mall on September 22, 1940. Money for the statue came from the George Robert White Fund.[87]

In the 1930s, the Italians began to win public office. Joe Langone Jr. was elected to the Massachusetts State Senate (1932), Edward Bacigalupo to the Massachusetts House of Representatives (1940) and Joe Russo to the Boston City Council (1939). Italians were finally beginning to come to political power.[88]

In the 1940s, soldiers were stationed in Christopher Columbus High School, which had been temporarily converted to barracks.

Significant Italian philanthropy began too. Born in 1863, John Deferrari began work as a fruit merchant. Business prospered. He made a fortune in real estate and the stock market. He was a devoted user of the Boston Public Library and in 1947 formed a foundation to give $1 million to the library. The main hall of the new building was named Deferrari Hall.

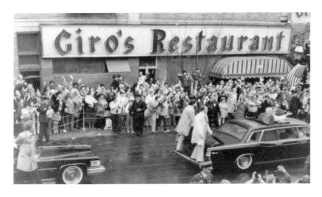

The pope's visit to the North End, 1979. *Vito Aluia collection.*

His family home on Wesley Place is located directly behind the northeast branch of the library.[89]

NORTH END GAINED NATIONAL PROMINENCE

In the 1960s, the North End was a safe neighborhood. In *The Death and Life of Great American Cities*, Jane Jacobs gave the North End national prominence as a model of city life. In response to Jane Jacobs's publicity, Boston Redevelopment Authority officials acknowledged the North End as one of the liveliest neighborhoods in Boston and assured residents no West End–like destruction would occur. Prominence became a challenge to the North End. North Enders became aware of the image they projected to the world. Tourists and Bostonians were descending on the area not just to view the historic buildings but eager to sample this paragon of community living.[90]

By the 1960s, however, many North End tenements were in need of physical repair or upgrade. The Home Owners' Loan Corporation (HOLC) maps show the North End was redlined (refused loans to renovate) in the 1930s and remained so until the 1970s. Over 30 percent of the tenements in 1960 were classified as "deteriorated" and 5 percent as "dilapidated." In the 1970s, more than half of the North End tenements did not have showers. Toilets were located in the hallways, often without sinks and often shared with other tenants on the floor. Many buildings had at least one vacancy because of the outflow of Italian Americans to the suburbs. That also meant Italian immigrants could find an apartment when they arrived.[91]

Physical deterioration was accompanied by social decline. In the 1980s, the North End was a poor neighborhood. Rebellion against parental authority at home was accompanied by rebellion against the government and police and the criminal network in the neighborhood. There was a significant increase in drug addiction, drug-related crimes and drug wars. There was a steady decline in overall population in the North End in the 1980s and 1990s as many Italian Americans moved out and Italian immigration diminished.[92]

Gentrification began in the 1970s. The gentrification of the North End contained a paradox. Its economic success meant it was important to market the North End as an Italian neighborhood even though the number of Italian American residents had greatly diminished.

The North End was at the beginning of the next phase of its evolution. It had retained the Italian cultural identity even as it had lost many Italians.

4

CULTURAL CRACKS IN THE NORTH END

ITALIANS VERSUS IRISH

The population of the North End transformed itself from Yankee to Irish to Irish-Jewish-Italian to Italian. In the overlap between the transformation from Irish to Italian, conflict abounded. The Italians felt they were treated badly by the Irish. The Irish were in the North End first and resented the intrusion of the Italians (most of them southern), whom they considered to be an inferior people, as they were largely illiterate. Although both the Irish and the Italians were Catholic, the Italians' language, customs and dress were incomprehensible to the Irish.[93]

The conflict between the Irish and the Italians did not start in the North End of Boston. It began in Europe—in Italy and in Ireland. At the heart of the dispute was Catholicism itself. Each viewed the Church differently. The Italians did not financially support the Catholic Church in America, partly because in Italy they did not have to pay to attend church, as the church was supported by the government. The Italians manifested a deep anticlericalism that was rooted in the conditions in Italy. Since the Italian unification movement of the 1860s, it had become difficult for an Italian in Italy to be both a loyal patriot and a devout Catholic. In Italy, the church formed an integral part of life. In America, the Italians found the church to be a cold, remote, puritanical institution staffed even in the North End by the Irish. They resisted the Irish domination of the church and wanted Italian priests.[94]

When the Irish arrived in the North End, they were as poor as the Italians. Time was on their side, however, and they had significantly improved their lot in life by the time the Italians arrived. The Irish also had a tremendous advantage with their ability to speak and understand English. The Italian and Irish immigrants competed for jobs and places to live.

At the time of the great immigration of the Italians, Irish "tough boys" controlled the street corners and barrooms. These were meeting places, and the Irish looked at these as their personal property. If they did not like the looks or actions of trespassers, they felt they had the right to take affairs into their own hands—physically.

The first Italians in the North End were the Genoese, and Genoese mothers walked their children to school to protect them from their Irish schoolmates. In the 1860s, there were times when it was dangerous for Italians to venture outside the neighborhood—even during the day. If there was an "incident," the Irish gangs would attack anyone in the territory. Even in the 1870s, the Genoese were dramatically restricted at night. Some of the tougher Irish lurked in the doorways of North Street, then a prominent center for dance halls and bars, and robbed drunks and took money from the Italians as they returned from work. It was for these reasons the early Genoese immigrants had nothing do with the Irish.[95]

This changed with the second generation. Many second-generation Genoese men became friendly with Irish girls. Genoese girls were strictly supervised by their parents. This forced the men to look to other races, and they would go to dance halls in other sections of Boston—South Boston, East Boston and Charlestown—to meet and dance with Irish girls.[96]

By the time the southern Italians flooded in—1880s, 1890s and early 1900s—the Genoese had gradually adapted to American customs, learned English and were moving to other areas. The southern Italians who came in were illiterate and clung to the customs and clothing of the villages they came from. They had difficulty adjusting, and the Irish turned their aggression to the southern Italians. Street fighting became hazardous. The southern Italians were peaceable until there was a fight, and then, as in the old country, they took out knives.[97]

The Irish fought differently. Street fighting was a sport with unwritten but clearly understood rules. Accepted weapons were fists, feet, brass knuckles, blackjacks, sticks, stones, bricks, bottles and other blunt instruments—but not knives or guns. Knives and guns were strictly banned. For the Irish, the purpose was to beat up the opponent with bruises and welts, but it was against the rules to kill or seriously injure. The Irish were shocked when the southern Italians used knives. In a fight with a knife, if the Irish combatant was able to disarm his opponent, the beating the knife wielder took was severe. In a strange way, the introduction of knives to street fighting brought an end to the sport of street fighting.[98]

Until 1915, Irish gangs controlled the waterfront. Walking during the day was safe. At night, the Irish would gather on street corners, and it would be dangerous for an Italian or a Jew to walk through their territory. Many Sicilian fishermen slept in their boats rather than risk the walk home.[99]

As the Irish improved their lot in life and moved out of the North End, the racial tension changed, and fighting no longer happened in the North End. It became the North End Italians versus the Irish in a different section of Boston—Charlestown.[100]

BLACK HAND AND THE MAFIA

With the Italian great immigration into Boston's North End also came Italian gang violence—the Black Hand and the Mafia. Americans feared these criminal organizations. Their existence led to increased discrimination against the Italians in America.

In the early 1900s, newspapers in the United States increasingly reported on a phenomenon known as the "Black Hand." The Black Hand sent threatening notes or letters printed with black hands to local merchants and the well-to-do, extorting money on pain of death or destruction of property. A Black Hand letter sometimes included a symbol of death—a drawing of skull and crossbones or a dagger. It promised to kill the recipient and his or her family if they did not follow the instructions in the letter. In March 1909, the *Boston Globe* reported that several businessmen in the North End and the West End were being targeted by the Black Hand. In 1911, Gaspare Poleo, who lived in the West End (which abutted the North End), where he operated a fruit and produce store in the building where he and his family lived, received a Black Hand letter that stated:

> *It is expected you will deliver $2,000 into the hands of a man you will meet on the Cambridge side, near the Porter Station on Sunday. The man you meet will be dressed in a light cap and wear a red handkerchief. You wear a dark hat and a red handkerchief. Do not delay very long in attending*

*to this. You do not belong to your miserable kind. If you do not tend to this,
you and your wife will suffer death.
Signed, The Black Hand*

At the bottom of the letter a skull and crossbones were drawn in ink. The letter had been mailed from the Hanover Street Post Office in the North End. Poleo did not comply with the letter, and on March 16, 1911, his home was bombed and destroyed. Both Poleo and his family escaped.

It was thought that the Black Hand, a precursor to the Mafia, was run in America by Sicilian and Italian gangsters from 1890 to 1920. This, of course, led to fear of the Italians and discrimination against them. In reality, the Black Hand was not an organized crime syndicate. Its letters were written by people of all different ethnicities and races.[101]

In August 1904, George Scigliano, a prominent attorney and the first man of Italian heritage born in Boston to be elected to the Massachusetts House of Representatives, achieved near-legendary status when he publicly stated he would ignore death threats from the mysterious Black Hand criminal organization and defy its demands that he resign as chairman of a local vigilance committee. The committee, composed of prominent Italians, was formed in the North End, Scigliano said,

To aid the police in hunting down a gang of Italian and Sicilian thugs who infested the lower part of the city…we are going to purge the city of Italian criminals. From some of the lurid accounts given by sensational newspapers, it might be thought that all Italians went around looking for plunder and blood. Of course, there is a criminal class that comes from our land as well as any other European country. I think, though, that the percentage of evil doers from Italy is far less than from other countries. Be that as it may, we are determined to arrest Italian criminals and have them put in jail or expelled from the city as their degree of crime allows. The committee does this to protect the public and also in the interest of the respectable hard-working Italians here. There is a smaller percentage of Italians in Boston that would be far better behind prison bars than at large, and these we have determined shall receive their just desserts. They can threaten, cajole or plead but justice will be meted out to them.[102]

Scigliano publicly announced he would ignore death threats from the mysterious criminal organization. La Camorra publicly marked seven Boston men for death, including three police officers and Scigliano. The

Boston American newspaper printed La Camorra's warning:

> *Your death is at hand; your life shall be destroyed in a manner which will freeze the blood of those like yourself who are spies and friends of the police. You have betrayed your countrymen and you have tried to send them to prison. Now, this is the last notice you will receive, and unless you at once leave Boston, never to return, you will be killed.*[103]

The article continued,

> *It does not seem possible that this can be true in Boston. If law and order are to be supreme anywhere it seems it must be here, in the shadow of the gilt dome that has covered the lawmakers of the most lawful state in the Union. But down in the North End where dark doorways and dismal alleys shelter swarthy people whose deeds keep them in constant war with the police, strange things are said and done.*

Neighbors and citizens went to Scigliano's home to protect him.

By fighting against the Black Hand while at the same time reminding people publicly that those criminals did not represent the thousands of honest Italians in the North End, Scigliano gained credibility among Italians and non-Italians alike.[104]

In 1908, Gaetano D'Amato, the former president of the United Italian Societies, wrote in an article in the *North American Review*,

> *It is not strange, perhaps, that most Americans believe that a terrible organization named the Black Hand Society exists in Italy and is sending its members to establish branches for the purposes of plundering the United States, since nearly every newspaper in the country conveys that impression to its readers.*
>
> *Mr. Terence Powderly, Chief of the Division of Information for the Immigration Bureau declared in an interview with the* New York Sun *newspaper that he had learned in Italy that the Black Hand was organized for good. "An Italian who wrongs a woman and fails to right the wrong is practically driven from among his fellows. The black hand of ostracism is raised against him. The Black Hand in this country was prostituted and converted to ignoble purposes when transplanted to the United States.*[105]

D'Amato noted the "Black Hand" was scarcely heard of in Italy:

In the US the Black Hand Society is a myth in so far as it conveys the impression that an organization of Italian criminals exists in America or that the Camorra or the Mafia have been naturalized here. By reason of the laxity of the immigration laws, there have crept into this country some thousands of ex-convicts from Naples, Sicily and Calabria along with millions of honest and industrious Italians; and owing to the inefficiency of the police in various cities where these Italians are domiciled, the criminals among them are able to live by robbery, extortion, frequently accompanied by murder, their victims being the most helpless of fellow countrymen.

How many of these criminals there are in the United States is impossible for obvious reasons to estimate with any degree of accuracy....They are no more organized, however, than are the many thousands of lawbreakers of other nationalities in America.

An ex-convict cannot obtain a passport from Italy and sail to America on an Italian ship, but there is nothing to prevent his crossing the frontier and leaving from another port outside Italy to make his way. Many of the dangerous Italians who came here came in through England or Canada.

During my 29 years of residence in New York, I have found two causes that operate for the blackening of the Italian name. In the respect of crime—the sensationalism of the yellow press and the ignorance and recklessness of the policy in recording arrests. Almost every dark skinned European, not speaking English, who does not wear the Turkish fez, is put down in the police records as Italian and therefore the Italian is condemned for much of the crime committed here by persons of other nationalities.

The term Black Hand is of Spanish, not Italian, origin and was first described in Spain in 1889. The term Black Hand was first used here in America 10 years ago, probably by some Italian desperado who had heard of the exploits of the Spanish society and considered the combination of the two words to be high-sounding and terror-inspiring.

The Black Hand incidents made good press and the press facilitates the commission of crime among the Italian ex-convicts by making it appear that all evil done by them is the successful work of a single organization that aids the individual criminal by leading his ignorant countrymen upon whom he preys to believe that he makes his lawless demands on behalf of a powerful society.[106]

Charles Ponzi

And then there was the infamous swindler and crook Charles Ponzi, who contributed to the mistrust of Italians.[107] In the 1920s, Charles Ponzi, who was born in Italy, became a North End resident and married Rose Marie Gnecco, a stenographer, whose father owned a small fruit stall. (He had been previously jailed and did not tell Rose. However, his mother wrote Rose a letter telling her about Ponzi's past, and she married him anyway.) Ponzi founded and operated a business, the Securities Exchange Company, initially on Hanover Street and later on School Street in Boston. He promised to double investments through a financial scheme involving postal coupons and exchange rates. In early 1920, his initial eighteen investors invested a total of $1,800. As business began to pick up, he hired agents and paid them a commission. By March 1920, his total investment had increased to $20,000, and by June people had invested $2.5 million. He was collecting $1 million a week and by the end of July $1 million a day.

He began to deposit the money in Hanover Trust of Boston (a bank on Hanover Street). People were mortgaging their homes and investing life savings. He did double their money, but he did it by paying them from funds other investors put in.

A Boston financial writer suggested there was no way he could legally produce such high returns in such a short period of time. Ponzi sued the financial writer for libel and won $500,000 in damages. Libel law at the time placed the burden of proof on the writer and publisher. On July 24, 1920, the *Boston Post* published a favorable article, and more investors came.

Ponzi moved from the North End to a mansion at 19 Slocum Road, Lexington, Massachusetts, and commuted to Boston each day in a chauffeured Bentley. When a reporter asked Ponzi about history's great Italians, he noted Christopher Columbus had discovered America and that Guglielmo Marconi had invented the radio.

"And Ponzi discovered money!" shouted an enthusiastic investor.

Helen Luongo stated:

> *My mother skimped and scraped to get the money together to go to the Ponzi office and as she was going on Hanover Street she met people who were saying that he had failed. You used to deposit the money for one month and he would give you 10, 12 percent and everybody went. Well, the first one who deposited and took the money, well, it's all right. But the last ones. He*

Charles Ponzi (*center, standing*). *North End Historical Society.*

ran off with the money! I'd call him a loan shark. I wouldn't call him a banker because [he] *only had a store as an office.*[108]

Arthur Barron, editor of an investment newsletter (now Barron's), criticized Ponzi's method. No investment could double in ninety days, and he also charged that an Italian immigrant like Ponzi could not understand the intricacies of capitalism.

Ponzi replied that Italians had invented banking. The ethnic slur against the Italians brought in more investors.

Two Boston police officers came to Ponzi's office to check his credentials, and they left as investors. But his scheme collapsed. His press agent (Ponzi was one of the first to hire a publicist) began to wonder why if Ponzi's investments returned 100 percent interest he kept his money in banks that paid only 5 percent interest. *Boston Post* acting publisher Richard Grozier became increasingly suspicious and assigned an investigative reporter to look into Ponzi's past and learned that the years he had spent in Montreal, where he claimed to have studied international finance, were years he had actually been in prison for check fraud. At the same time, the state began an investigation into Ponzi, and he was able to derail it by telling the investigators he would not take any additional investment money while the probe was continuing.

The *Boston Post* ramped up its articles and asked pointed questions—such as why Ponzi was not investing his own money. As the investigative reporting made it clearer and clearer that there were significant questions, there was a panic run and all it crashed down.[109]

Ponzi was indicted at the federal level on eighty-six counts of mail fraud, faced life imprisonment, pleaded guilty at his wife's insistence and was sentenced to five years in prison.

The *Boston Post* won a Pulitzer Prize for its investigation. Six banks that had lent money to Ponzi collapsed. Thousands of investors (mostly immigrants) who had mortgaged their homes or turned their life savings over to Ponzi were ruined. Approximately $20 million was lost. He went to jail again and was deported to Italy.[110]

Ponzi was released from prison after three and a half years and was indicted by Massachusetts on twenty-two charges of larceny. He argued double jeopardy, and his case, *Ponzi v. Fessenden*, went to the U.S. Supreme Court, which ruled on March 27, 1922, that federal plea bargains had no standing regarding state charges and he did not face double jeopardy because Massachusetts charged him with larceny while the federal government charged him with mail fraud. In October 1922, Ponzi served as his own attorney in the first larceny case and was acquitted by a jury. In the second larceny case, the jury was deadlocked. He was found guilty in the third larceny case and was sentenced to seven to nine years in prison as "a common and notorious thief." Ponzi was released on bail and fled to Florida, where he swindled landowners. He was sent back to Massachusetts to finish his jail term.

He was released from prison in 1934 and deported to Italy. His wife divorced him. He wrote his own biography, *Charles Ponzi: The Rise and Fall of Mr. Ponzi* (1936). Ponzi granted one last interview to an American reporter, telling him, "Even if they never got anything for it, it was cheap at that price. Without malice aforethought, I had given them the best show that was ever staged in their territory since the landing of the Pilgrims! It was easily worth fifteen million bucks to watch me put the thing over."

Charles Ponzi died in a charity hospital in Rio de Janeiro on January 15, 1949, at age sixty-six. His swindling legacy has been continued by Victor Lustig (the Austria-Hungarian scam artist who "sold the Eiffel Tower twice"), Arthur Nadel (American hedge fund swindler) and of course, Bernie Madoff.

THE MAFIA

The Mafia, or Cosa Nostra, started in Sicily. The FBI notes the first major Mafia incident on American soil occurred in New Orleans in October 1890. Police Chief David Hennessey was murdered in a Mafia-related incident. This made the public aware of the Mafia and afraid of the Mafia.[111]

The following week, Massachusetts representative Henry Cabot Lodge published an article in the *North American Review* in which he defended the lynch mob and proposed his new restrictions on immigration.[112]

On July 21, 1895, the *Boston Sunday Post* asserted that the Mafia existed in Boston and that Boston was central headquarters for the Mafia in New England. The *Post* stated that not every Italian was a Mafioso and the Mafia's numbers were small in proportion to Boston's Italian population, but it opined it was safe to say that of the southern Italians and especially the Sicilians, every other one was either a Mafia member or in sympathy with the organization. The *Post* estimated there were two hundred Mafia members in Boston.[113]

In 1903, the *Post* wrote that the Mafia "is a name the sound of which strikes terror to the hearts of some of the people of the North End."[114]

The Mafia officially arrived in the North End in 1915 with Gaspara Messina, originally from Sicily, who moved his family from New York and became one of the earliest mob bosses in Boston. By 1925, he was operating a wholesale grocery business, G. Messina & Company, at 28½ Prince Street. He was also president of the Neptune Oil Company. In 1930, he was selected to serve as the Mafia's *capo dei capi*, the boss of bosses. He and his partner ran a very successful lottery and bootlegging operation on Hanover Street.[115]

Not all the big criminals in the North End were Italian. In 1932, a group of gangsters and racketeers met at Hotel Manger at 76 Causeway Street at the edge of the North End for a secret meeting to discuss how to control the pool and lottery tickets. They were busted by the police. One of the members, Dr. Harry Sagansky (who was Jewish not Italian), was known as the "kingpin in Boston," and it is estimated his numbers pulled in $8 million a year. He graduated from Tufts Dental in 1918 and started off as a dentist but found bookmaking far more lucrative. He made a fortune. In 1963, he established the Dr. Harry Sagansky Fellowship Fund to subsidize tuition for graduate students at Brandeis. He also ran a loan agency. In the 1950s, an investigatory committee led by U.S. senator Estes Kefauver listed Sagansky as among the top bookies in the country.[116]

The Mafia hit hard times in the North End. In the summer of 1964, Sandro Bartone, an Italian immigrant, took a job at Stella's restaurant on Fleet Street and became very friendly with the Anguilo family. The Anguilos were born and raised in the North End and controlled the biggest gaming operation in Boston. Unknown to the Anguilos, Bartone was actually an undercover agent for the U.S. government whose real name was Sante Bario. He infiltrated the inner circle of the North End Mafia, leading to one of the biggest IRS busts. On November 1, 1965, agents descended on the North End and raided places on Endicott, Commercial, Hanover and Margin Streets, arresting twenty-three people.[117]

The Anguilos lived on Prince Street and operated their business from that locale. In 1981, federal agents raided 91, 95 and 98 Prince Street and confiscated a safe that contained more than $300,000. Gennaro "Jerry" Angiulo was a regular in the back room of Francesca's Restaurant at 90 North Washington Street. In 1983, he was taken out of the restaurant in handcuffs. After an eight-month trial, he was convicted of racketeering, gambling, loan sharking and obstruction of justice in 1986 and sentenced to forty-five years in prison. He was paroled in 2007. He died two years later at age ninety.[118]

Today, within the North End, the Mafia is perceived as at worst harmless and at best beneficial.

Some believe that the Mafia actually held the North End neighborhood together, that organized crime preserved the neighborhood. The "eyes on the street" that preserved the North End were not those of the passersby or shoppers. Rather, the most influential sidewalk spectators were part of Boston's strongest criminal force—the mob. The Patriarca family oversaw the North End and ensured it was protected by a highly networked community of Mafioso. It protected the North End community from ordinary street crime in exchange for anonymity. It created and invested in legitimate businesses—clubs, restaurants and bakeries. Knowing the investments were made by the Mafia caused ordinary criminals to detour from the neighborhood.[119]

Commenting on the death of the last surviving North End mobster, Frank Anguilo, attorney Anthony Cardinale, who represented Anguilo's brother, stated,

"Unlike rival South Boston gangster James 'Whitey' Bulger, who raked in millions by flooding his own neighborhood with drugs, the Anguilos tried to keep drugs out of the North End. These guys really made sure the neighborhood was safe. No one would ever think of breaking into an apartment or robbing a store or doing anything when they were there. They had that kind of impact." The Anguilos made money mostly from bookmaking and loan sharking. Still, they were convicted in a sweeping federal racketeering case that included brutal murders.[120]

A lifelong North End resident, Mike Tirella believed the North End was safer when the Anguilos were around. "The Anguilos weren't a bad name when I was growing up. I don't think they bothered people in the North End. I think they helped a lot of people."[121]

ANARCHY

By 1915, the Italian anarchist national headquarters and center of operations was in the North End. Anarchists had frightened Americans for a long time. In 1916, on New Year's morning in Boston, a Massachusetts State House night watchman making his rounds discovered a wicker suitcase tied to a doorknob at the sergeant-at-arms's office. Inside was dynamite, which did not ignite because of a faulty fuse. The next morning, an explosion ripped apart the New England Manufacturing Company in Woburn (a Boston suburb). Rumors quickly circulated that the company had received a letter two weeks earlier threatening to blow up the plant or set fire to it unless it stopped producing goods and shipping them overseas to warring nations in Europe.[122]

In 1916, Boston police issued warnings that the North End had become the headquarters for some of the leading anarchists in America, whose tools were terror and violence. Years of poverty and government oppression in Italy had incited the anti-government, anti-capitalism passion of Italian anarchists and driven some to radical acts. As anarchist Nicola Sacco put it, "The plight of the working class is poverty and squalor in the midst of plenty."[123]

Historian Paul Avrich pointed out that "the Italian anarchists (like Sacco) were in the end sure that truth, justice, and freedom would triumph over falsehood, tyranny and oppression. To accomplish this however would require a social revolution, for only a complete overthrow of the existing social order, the abolition of property and the destruction of the state, would bring the 'final emancipation of the worker.'"[124]

On December 16, 1917, an early morning dynamite bomb explosion ripped a hole in the three-foot-thick brick wall of the Salutation Street police station, breaking every window on one side of the building, blowing out window sashes and splitting the window casings. The bomb was placed in the jail cell in the basement directly under rooms in which three policemen were sleeping. The policemen escaped unharmed. The force of the eighteen to twenty dynamite sticks substantially damaged neighboring buildings. Italian anarchists claimed credit for the bombing—retaliation against Boston police for the arrests of several anarchists after a violent anti–military preparedness riot in North Square.[125]

That same year, Luigi Galleani, a Boston anarchist, was labeled by the Justice Department as the "leading anarchist in the United States." He was the publisher of a newspaper, *Cronaca Souversiva* (Subversive Chronicle), that the Justice Department called "the most rabid, seditious and anarchistic sheet ever published in this country." He was charged with conspiracy to obstruct the draft, entered a plea of guilty and was ordered to pay a $300 fine.[126]

SACCO AND VANZETTI

Anarchy continued in Boston with the arrest of Nicola Sacco and Bartolomeo Vanzetti in the 1920s. Sacco and Vanzetti were Italian immigrant anarchists who were accused of murdering a guard and paymaster during the April 15, 1920 armed robbery of the Slater and Morrill Shoe Company in Braintree, Massachusetts.

On July 14, 1921, after a few hours of deliberation, a jury convicted Sacco and Vanzetti of first-degree murder and they were sentenced to death. At that time, first-degree murder in Massachusetts was punishable by death. Supporters believed that Sacco and Vanzetti had been convicted for their anarchist views, yet every juror insisted that anarchism did not play a part in the judgment.

The Sacco and Vanzetti Defense Committee (privately funded with $300,000) funded a series of appeals.[127]

The appeals were based on recanted testimony, conflicting ballistics evidence, a prejudicial pretrial statement by the jury foreman and a confession by an alleged participant in the robbery. Trial judge Webster Thayer and later the Massachusetts Supreme Judicial Court denied all appeals.

Sacco and Vanzetti wrote dozens of letters asserting their innocence. From a typed letter of Nicola Sacco and Bartolomeo Vanzetti to the Delegate of the United Mine Workers Convention, Indianapolis, Indiana:

We are not afraid to die. Every worker in the performance of his tasks as an industrial serf faces death a thousand times. Death we do not fear. We do revolt against having our heartbeats stopped for a crime we did not commit, indeed for a crime that possesses no industrial or social significance.

From our earliest days of our young manhood up to the time of our arrest, we gave unsparingly of our time, our labor, and the money we earned by hard labor to the education of the workers, preparatory to the day when the workers might emancipate themselves. We are not the type of men who steal and murder. No man who is in a normal mental condition ever commits murder. Crimes of force prove conclusively that there is some diseased condition existing in society. It is a symptom of individual and social maladjustment.

There is no need for us to retell the story upon which our conviction was built. A fine network of lies was built and innocent acts of ours were contorted by the vicious minds of those who say the champions of labor are only the "enemies of the people." American capitalism cannot understand

Sacco and Vanzetti. *Boston Public Library*.

that a man can be an unafraid fighter against exploitation and at the same time have a mind.[128]

In 1926, the Sacco and Vanzetti case had worldwide attention. In 1927, protests were held on their behalf in every major city in North America as well as Tokyo, Sydney, Melbourne, São Paulo, Rio de Janeiro, Buenos Aires, Dubai, Johannesburg and Auckland.[129]

Future U.S. Supreme Court justice Felix Frankfurter argued for their innocence in an *Atlantic Monthly* article that later became a book.[130]

American author and journalist John Dos Passos joined the Defense Committee and wrote its 127-page official review of the case.[131]

Dos Passos concluded it was "barely possible" that Sacco might have committed murder but that the soft-hearted Vanzetti was clearly innocent. "Nobody in their right mind who was planning such a crime would take a man like that along."

Dos Passos, working as a journalist, was arrested in a demonstration on August 10, 1927, along with Dorothy Parker, trade union organizer;

Sacco and Vanzetti protest. *Boston Public Library*.

Socialist Party leader Powers Hapgood; and activist Catharine Sargent Huntington.[132]

Poet Edna St. Vincent Millay was arrested while picketing the statehouse and made a personal plea to the governor:

Your Excellency

…Tonight, with the world in doubt, with this Commonwealth drawing into its lungs with every breath the difficult air of doubt, with the eyes of Europe turned westward upon Massachusetts and upon the whole United States in distress and harrowing doubt—are you still so sure? Does not faintest shadow of question gnaw at your mind? For, indeed, your spirit, however strong, is but the frail spirit of a man. Have you no need, in this hour, of a spirit greater than your own?

Think back. Think back a long time. Which way would He have turned, this Jesus of your faith?—Oh, not the way in which your feet are set!

You promised me, and I believed you truly, that you would think of what I said. I exact of you this promise now. Be for a moment alone with yourself. Look inward upon yourself. Let fall from your harassed mind all, all save this: which way would He have turned, this Jesus of your faith?

I cry to you with a million voices: answer our doubt. Exert the clemency which your high office affords.

There is need in Massachusetts of a great man tonight. It is not yet too late for you to be that man.

Edna St. Vincent Millay

On April 7, 1927, Judge Thayer heard final statements. In his, Bartolomeo Vanzetti said,

I would not wish a dog or a snake, the most low and misfortuned creature of the earth. I would not wish to any of them what I have had to suffer for things that I am not guilty of. But my conviction is that I have suffered for things I am guilty of. I am suffering because I am a radical, and indeed I am a radical. I have suffered because I am an Italian, and indeed I am an Italian.…If you could execute me two times and if I could be reborn two more times, I would live again to do what I have already done.[133]

Due to the public outcry, Governor Alvan T. Fuller faced last-minute appeals to grant clemency. On June 1, 1927, he appointed an advisory committee of three: President Abbott Lawrence Lowell of Harvard, President Samuel Wesley Stratton of MIT and Probate Judge Robert Grant. In the court appeals, the defense had been limited to the trial record. This was not a court proceeding, so the committee could listen to other comments, including the outspoken comments of Judge Thayer, who called Sacco and Vanzetti anarchist bastards. The committee met for two weeks and determined the trial was fair and a new trial was not warranted.[134]

The executions were scheduled for midnight between August 22 and 23, 1927. On August 15, a bomb exploded at the home of one of the jurors. On August 21, more than twenty thousand protestors assembled on the Boston Common.[135] The Boston Italians—who for the most part opposed anarchists and anarchy—overwhelmingly supported Sacco and Vanzetti, not because they sympathized with the cause but because they believed the convicted murderers sat on Death Row not because they were guilty but because they were Italian. Sacco and Vanzetti were executed in 1927. They lay in state in the North End's Langone Funeral Home for two days, and thousands paid their respects. For the most part, anarchy ended in the North End with their execution.

Dos Passos's stark poem "They Are Dead Now" captures the mood of the time:

> THEY ARE DEAD NOW
> A EULOGY FOR SACCO AND VANZETTI
> This isn't a poem
> This is two men in grey prison clothes.
> One man sits looking at the sick flesh of his hands—hands that haven't
>   worked for seven years
> Do you know how long a year is?
> Do you know how many hours there are in a day
> when a day is twenty-three hours on a cot in a cell,
> in a cell in a row of cells in a tier of rows of cells
> all empty with the choked emptiness of dreams?
> Do you know the dreams of men in jail?
> They are dead now
> The black automatons have won.
> They are burned up utterly
> their flesh has passed into the air of Massachusetts their dreams have
>   passed into the wind.
> "They are dead now," the Governor's secretary nudges the Governor,

"They are dead now," the Superior Court Judge nudges the Supreme Court
    Judge,
"They are dead now," the College President nudges the College President
A dry chuckling comes up from all the dead:
The white collar dead; the silkhatted dead;
the frockcoated dead
They hop in and out of automobiles
breathe deep in relief
as they walk up and down the Boston streets.
they are free of dreams now
free of greasy prison denim
their voices blow back in a thousand lingoes
singing one song
to burst the eardrums of Massachusetts
Make a poem of that if you dare![136]

This case led to judicial reform in Massachusetts. In December 1927, four months after the executions, the Massachusetts Judicial Council cited this case as evidence of "serious defects in our methods of administering justice." Its principal point was that not any one judge should have borne the burden in a capital case. The Massachusetts Supreme Judicial Court should have the right to review. A review could defend a judge whose decisions were challenged and make it less likely a governor would be drawn into the case. It asked the Supreme Judicial Court to have the right to order a new trial "upon any ground if the interests of justice appear to inquire it." Governor Fuller endorsed this.[137] The judicial council repeated its recommendations in 1937 and 1938. In 1939, the language was adopted, and since then, the Massachusetts Supreme Judicial Court has been required to review all death penalty cases, to consider the entire case record and to affirm or overturn the verdict on the law and on the evidence or "for any other reason that justice may require."[138]

On August 23, 1977, fifty years later, Massachusetts governor Michael Dukakis issued a proclamation that Sacco and Vanzetti had been unfairly tried and convicted and that "any disgrace should be forever removed from their names." He did, however, stop short of proclaiming them innocent.[139] In 1997, Thomas Menino, Boston's first Italian American mayor, and acting governor Paul Cellucci formally accepted on behalf of the city a bas-relief sculpture memorializing Sacco and Vanzetti. The piece, created by Gutzon Borglum (of Mount Rushmore fame) had been repeatedly offered as a gift to the city and rejected. In 1937, Massachusetts governor Charles Hurley called it "a patently absurd gesture," while Boston mayor Frederick Mansfield said it had "no possible chance of acceptance." It was rejected again in 1947 and 1957. The piece now hangs in the Special Collections lobby of the Boston Public Library. It shows the two men in profile with a quote from Vanzetti's final prison letter.[140]

DISCRIMINATION AND DEPORTATION

As has been illustrated throughout this book, for many decades, discrimination against the Italians was strong in America. The discrimination was not just in Boston and not just in the North End—it was throughout America. The aura of discrimination was pervasive. Incidents that happened elsewhere in the country reverberated, and the consequences were very much in existence in the North End.

Following the lynching of 11 Italians in New Orleans in 1891, 1,500 Boston Italians with "coal black hair and eyes" (according to the *Boston Globe*) gathered in Faneuil Hall to protest and demand reparations. One of the speakers, Dr. Brindisi, urged the audience to be calm. "Italians be calm: Don't get excited. Trust to the authorities of this government to see that justice will be done."[141]

FEDERAL STREET RIOTS

In August 1905, two hundred members of the North End's Liguaria Society were parading down Federal Street when a trolley car driver refused to stop for them. Several "young ruffians" jumped out of the car and "set upon" the driver and the conductor, breaking windows and sending the passengers fleeing in terror. The fight, in which the conductor's nose was broken, "created a sensation" in Boston and became known as the "Federal Street Riot of 1905."[142]

The anti-immigrant sentiment had been building, and it escalated during the 1920s. Italians appear to have been as productive as any other workers. Police arrest records indicate nothing unusual in the number of Italians involved in crime. And yet they faced discrimination in housing and employment and police brutality. Then there were the suspicions about ties to terrorism. Anti-capitalism anarchism frightened many and was tied in the popular mind to the Italians.

THE RED SCARE AND DEPORTATION

The first American Red Scare of 1919–20 resulted in the deportation of Italians whom Americans saw as being political radicals.[143] Activists, like Red Scare perpetrators, identified deportation as a newly important weapon. But unlike their opponents, they saw it as a weapon that would encroach on the aims of American laws, rather than uphold them. As the Workers' Defense Union said when discussing the expulsion of a member, "The forces of greed have found in the deportation laws a whip of effectiveness against dissatisfied foreign workers. The prospect of exile is constantly before the men and women who demand a larger share of what they produce."[144]

In the 1920s, a bombing on Wall Street was blamed on Italians, and as a result, five hundred Italians were deported back to Italy even though guilt was never proven. A man drove a cart and horse in front of the U.S. Assay Office across from the JP Morgan Building on Wall Street. The driver got out and disappeared into the crowd. The cart exploded into a hail of metal fragments, killing thirty and injuring three hundred. The chief clerk of JP Morgan, William Joyce, was killed. Junius Morgan, son of JP Morgan, was injured.[145]

The New York Police and Fire Departments, the Bureau of Investigation (precursor to the FBI) and the U.S. Secret Service investigated. Hundreds were interviewed. The bomb was reconstructed. No one took credit for the bombing. The most promising lead came before the explosion. A letter carrier had found four crudely spelled and printed flyers in the area from a group calling itself the "American Anarchist Fighters" that demanded the release of political prisoners. After three years of leads, the mystery was not solved. The best evidence and analysis since that date (September 16, 1920) indicated the bureau's initial thought was correct—that a small group of Italian Americans were to blame—but the mystery remains.[146]

With no explanations, the press and the public clamored for answers. Attorney General A. Mitchell Palmer instituted what became known as the "Palmer Raids" and ordered the rounding up and deporting of as many radicals as they could. As many as ten thousand immigrants were swept up in the raids, although fewer than five hundred were actually deported.[147]

Fear against the immigrants continued in the 1920s. Incidents in Chicago separated by nearly ninety years demonstrate the persistence of racially based enforcement of deportation law. In a 1925 deportation drive in Chicago, purportedly carried out to clean up Sicilian organized crime and rid the city of dangerous mobsters, the Chicago Police Department raided the Italian immigrant neighborhoods for weeks, picking up hundreds, including women and children. When detainees were turned over to the immigration officials to determine if they were deportable, agents found large numbers of Greek and Mexican people lumped in by their skin tone and residential proximity. While most of the detainees, Italian or otherwise, were ultimately not deportable, the raids and the smaller number of actual deportations met their more critical goal of terrorizing and controlling immigrant communities.[148]

The push for deportation escalated during the 1920s (building on the anti-immigrant sentiment that had been building since the 1880s). During World War II, the United States saw Italian Americans as threat to homeland security. Executive Order 9066 allowed the government to arrest and imprison "enemy aliens" without charges or trial and allowed their homes and businesses to be seized. On the West Coast, California's attorney general Earl Warren (later the chief justice of the United States) was relentless in registering aliens for detention.

After Mussolini declared war on the United States, Italians in Boston were anxious to prove their loyalty to their adopted country. Prominent Italians condemned Mussolini's actions, and young Italians rushed to enlist in the U.S. military. The navy was a popular option for Boston Italians, many of whom were fishermen. There was also a rush to obtain citizenship, with thousands of mostly Italian immigrants descending on the immigration office within days of the announcement.[149]

Nonnaturalized Italians in Boston (and elsewhere) were declared "enemy aliens" in 1941. Many were older women who had not become citizens because of language or literacy issues, and many had one or more children enlisted in the service. The proclamation was especially hard on Boston's Italian fishermen, whose boats were beached in some cases or requisitioned for use as patrol boats and minesweepers.[150]

Only two Boston Italians were interned—both radio broadcasters. One, Vbaldo Guido, was a popular pro-fascist radio host in the 1930s.[151] When he was arrested, he had two sons in the military.[152]

Changing Perception of the Italians in America and Boston

After World War II, many Italian American veterans took advantage of the GI bill enabling them to go to college and buy homes in the suburbs.

One commentator suggests that the federal holiday honoring the Italian explorer Christopher Columbus was central to the process through which Italian Americans were fully ratified as white during the twentieth century. The rationale for the holiday was steeped in myth and allowed Italian Americans to write a laudatory portrait of themselves into the civic record.[153]

On Columbus Day 1942, President Franklin D. Roosevelt declared Italians were no longer to be considered enemy aliens.

After World War II, Italian Americans were no longer marginalized or discriminated against. As the Italian Americans increasingly assimilated into the American culture, the discrimination against them waned. They had changed their image and were accepted.

5
ITALIAN AMERICANS AND THE CATHOLIC CHURCH

B eing Catholic in America was different from being Catholic in Italy. In Italy, the unification had enhanced existing anticlericalism and freemasonry. Disastrous economic policies before and after unification had driven many into socialism or anarchism and, in their fight for bare existence, into religious indifference. Italians saw the Catholic Church as a wealthy institution whose priests managed to live in comfort while the peasants struggled.

BEING ITALIAN CATHOLIC IN AN IRISH CATHOLIC CITY: AN UNDERCURRENT OF ANTI-PAPAL AND ANTICLERICAL SENTIMENTS

In America (and in Boston in particular), the relationship between the Italian Catholics and the church created issues for the Italian Catholics. In Boston (and in other cities in which the Italians settled most densely), Irish Catholics dominated the church hierarchy. The Irish Catholics held an intense prejudice toward the king of Italy and his subjects. The source of this animosity was the encroachment on the temporal authority and domain of the papacy resulting from the unification of Italy. During the Risorgimento, the American Irish led by Archbishop John Hughes of New York raised funds and prayers for the defense of the Holy See. From the pulpit, anathemas were hurled at Garibaldi, Victor Emmanuel and their followers as despoilers of the patrimony of the church.[154]

Among the few thousand Italians in mid-nineteenth-century America were many political exiles who had participated in the ill-fated revolutionary uprisings of the 1830s and 1840s.[155]

Through organizations, publications and public meetings, these Italian patriots agitated vociferously on behalf of the unification of Italy; their strongest incentive was reserved for the papal power, which they regarded as the chief obstacle to the realization of their aspiration. Pius IX was himself attacked in *L'Unione Italiana* of Chicago.

"The Grand Tyrant, the butcher of liberty, the Father of the Faithful and the Heir of St. Peter who invokes the aid of bayonets in apparent defense of a religion by no one threatened and who has his foundation not in the blood of Martyrs but in greed for temporal dominion and hatred against the unity and liberty of Italy."[156]

The anti-papal propaganda reached a fever pitch with the arrival of Father Alessandro Gavassi, the "priest-hero" of the revolution of 1848, whose lectures touched off anti-Catholic riots. Gavassi and the Italian nationalists launched bitter attacks upon Monsignor Gaetano Bedini during his visit to the United States in 1854. They denounced the papal nuncio as the "Bloody of Bologna" who had committed atrocities against the revolutionaries. The announced intention of Italians and others to burn Bedini in effigy in front of the residence of Archbishop Hughes brought out hundreds of armed Irishmen to defend their prelate. The turmoil that accompanied Bedini's visit led the editor of the *Irish American* to comment that the mission of the Italian in America was aimed at exciting Protestant animosity against the Irish Catholics. For their part, the Italians were convinced that the Irish who succored the pope with money and men were religious fanatics and sworn enemies of la patria.[157]

The occupation of Rome by Italian troops on September 20, 1870, joyfully celebrated by the Italians in America, was to the American Catholics the act of supreme sacrilege.[158]

Pius IX and his successors refused to recognize the new Kingdom of Italy, forbade Catholic participation in political life and styled themselves "prisoners of the Vatican." This conflict between church and state had severe repercussions for the Italian immigrants. For the American Irish, the "Roman Question" caused a perennial state of hostility towards Italy and the Italians.[159]

From the pulpit, they were taught that Victor Emmanuel and Garibaldi were brigands who had stolen the papal domain. Many believed the pope was literally a prisoner in chains, sleeping on straw and living on crusts of bread. When the Italians appeared on the scene, it was to be expected that the Irish would greet the jailers of the Holy Father with brickbats rather than bouquets.[160]

Nor did the demeanor of the newcomers persuade the Irish that they were devout sons of the Mother Church. Unlike the Irish or the Poles, whose Catholicism was an integral part of their national identity, the Italians found it difficult to be both an Italian patriot and a faithful Catholic. It is important to note that there is a dual mission to American Catholicism. The immigrant must be faithful to his religion and must become a good American citizen.[161] Edmund M. Dunne, bishop of Peoria, wrote in an essay that the church was an essential vehicle for the education of foreigners: "She is the best qualified to weld into one democratic brotherhood, one great American citizenship, the children of various climes, temperaments, and conditions."[162]

Henry Steele Commager wrote, referring to the years after 1880, "It might indeed be maintained that the Catholic Church was, during the period, one of the most effective agencies for democracy and Americanization."[163]

The conservative role of the church in its relation to the immigrant proletariat has been reaffirmed recently with the claim that its teachings "closed the immigrant's ears to siren songs of radicalism or revolt."[164]

An aggressive anticlericalism became a powerful force in late nineteenth-century Italy as nationalist, liberal and socialist views prevailed. Such was particularly true of the educated classes, among whom, as Luigi Villani observed, "the rarest thing in the world is to meet a clerical."[165]

Taking part in the mass migration to America was an intellectual proletariat of doctors, teachers, journalists and scholars. Although a small minority, they occupied a strategic position in the political and cultural life of the Italian colonies. Through their publications and free-thought societies, they carried on anticlerical propaganda against their countrymen in America.

Although a few Catholic newspapers were published, the colonial press by and large championed the cause of united Italy and heaped abuse on the pope and his minions. These polemics sometimes took extreme rhetorical forms, as when L'Italia of Chicago exclaimed, "When Leo XII [sic, XIII] kneels before Christ He should let him have a blow which would knock him head over heels into hell."

The Italian radicals were the most extreme *mangiaprett* (literally "priest eaters"). Through journals they waged unrelenting warfare against the church and all its works.

An American priest indignantly reported, "Italian news shops of Chicago are ablaze with vile anticlerical literature and would display in the street windows gross caricatures of the Pope and the Bishops of the Church."[166]

The Italian intelligentsia formed Circolo Giordano Bruno, composed of professionals and businessmen whose objective was to liberate the Italian workers from "superstition and ignorance"—in other words, clerical domination. Its primary targets were Irish priests. On February 23, 1908, an Italian immigrant shot and killed a priest while he was serving communion in Denver, Colorado. The nation was horror-stricken by the act and responded with cries against the Italian anarchists. In Chicago, a terror swept the city as priests said Mass under police protection, especially in Italian churches.[167]

It is important to note that they were anticlerical and not necessarily anti-state anarchists.

The Giordano Bruno members were not daunted and charged Reverend Dunne, pastor of the Italian Church of the Guardian Angel in Chicago, with defaming the Italians because of hatred of "our race."

There was widespread antipathy against Italian immigrants, and the clash of religious cultures, Italian versus Irish, was prevalent in other cities, such as Chicago, too.

The Chicago delegation to the First Congress of Italians abroad stated: "We Italians are not religious enthusiasts; we are sincere, strong, anticlericals opposed to the temporal force of the church. For this reason, we are not well regarded in this country in which the power of the Church is reaching dangerous proportions, especially by the Irish element, which is a great majority in the United States and has made itself the defender of the Papacy and the Church."[168]

The Italian Problem

Anticlericalism was part of the Italian problem—but not its most significant part. Most Italian immigrants were not free thinkers or socialists; they were peasants, and the peasants were parochial and traditional.[169] Roman Catholicism in Italy, the peasant religion, was a folk religion, a fusion of Christian and pre-Christian elements of animism, polytheism and sorcery within sacraments of the church. The religion of the peasant was enclosed within the spirit of the *campanilismo* (a figure of speech suggesting the world of peasantry was confined within earshot of the village belfry). Each village had its own array of Madonnas, saints and assorted spirits to be venerated, propitiated or exorcised. There was no turn of fortune, for good or for ill, that was not due to the benevolence or malevolence of these supernatural beings. God, like the king, was a distant, unapproachable figure, but the local saints and Madonna, like the landlords, were real personages whose favor was of vital importance. With a mixture of piety and shrewdness, supplicants bargained with their patron saints, offering gifts, sacrifices and praise if their petitions were granted. (If the saint, however, failed to produce the desired result, his statue stood in danger of being cast out of the church.)[170]

For the church itself, the southern Italian peasants had little sense of reverence. Historically, it had been allied with the land-owning aristocracy and shown little sympathy for the peasants. Although surrounded by a multitude of clergy, the people by and large were not instructed in the fundamentals of the Catholic faith. Toward their village priests, whom they regarded as parasites living off their labors, the peasants often displayed attitudes of familiar contempt. Clerical immorality and greed figured largely in the folk humor of Italy. The parish priest appeared to be regarded as a functionary who performed the necessary rites of baptisms, marriages and funerals. Other than on these occasions and on feast days, the peasants, especially the men, rarely set foot in the church. The fact that the priests rarely accompanied their parishioners to America reflected the lack of reciprocal affection between the clergy and the people.[171]

The Italian peasants, to be sure, thought of themselves as Cristiani—but their brand of Christianity had little in common with American Catholicism. "The fact is the Catholic Church in America is to the mass of Italians almost like a new religion."[172]

The Italian Problem for the Irish Catholics in Boston

In Boston (and in the other cities in which the Italians migrated), all of this was the backdrop for the issues the Italian immigrants faced in their relationship to the Catholic Church.

Here, due at least partially to illiteracy, Italian religious education was poor, and regular church attendance was generally viewed as a female activity. In Italy, men attended church services on holy days and special family occasions. In America, both men and women were expected to attend church, and Catholics were expected to pay a seat offering when attending, as well as monetary offerings for baptisms and marriage ceremonies. In Italy, there was no charge for any of this; the government paid for it.[173]

The Italian immigrant was struggling financially and probably working seven days a week to move his family ahead. Paying to attend church was a foreign concept, so many of them did not attend. They did not understand that in America the Catholic Church was a business that had to sustain itself through financial support.[174]

The "Italian Problem" was many things to many people, but to the Italian immigrants themselves it may have been that the church in the United States was more American and Irish than Catholic.[175]

THE PERSPECTIVE OF THE BOSTON ARCHDIOCESE

In the three-volume *History of the Archdiocese of Boston, 1604–1942*, the authors noted that Italian immigrants posed an unusual problem for the Catholic Church. It was hard to draw them into normal contact with the church or to induce them to attend to their religious duties with the fidelity and regularity that American Catholics commonly showed. Many reports on this subject appeared in the Catholic press. The newcomers, it was said, did not even know the rudiments of their faith, had never received any instruction about their religious duties and had never received any sacrament, save baptism. Hardly one in one hundred, it was affirmed, attended Mass with any regularity, and most appeared to have abandoned their religion in the Bay of Naples. Those who had retained any religious sense seemed to express it only in emotionalism or in occasionally going to Mass for the feast of some national saint. There was even talk of "the apostasy en masse of the Italian immigrants."[176]

The authors of *The History of the Archdiocese* conceded that much of this talk was exaggerated or unduly pessimistic, applying chiefly to the early period of immigration. Nevertheless, there was a grave problem here. The vast majority of Italian immigrants were Catholic, either by education and conviction, or at least by tradition, custom or sentiment. Many were able to display a faith as ardent as any other group of American Catholics. However, the conditions they had known in Italy, combined with some of their early experiences in America, tended to imperil Catholic faith or practice. Back home, their religious instruction, especially in the rural parts of the South, had been somewhat neglected. When the immigrants first arrived in the United States, their ignorance of the language also led many to stay away from English-speaking churches.

In Italy, the clergy had received salaries from the government, so it was hard for Italian immigrants to adjust to the idea of paying money for marriage or baptisms or "seat money" at the door whenever they came to Mass. They were all too likely to conclude that the American clergy were money-mad or at least that religion in this country was too expensive for them.

Nothing would have helped smooth over the natural difficulties of the transition period more than the presence of an adequate supply of Italian priests who could speak the language and understand the needs of the immigrants, as no one else could. However, Italian priests had not come over to this country to serve their compatriots in anything like the numbers of clergy of other immigrant groups.

Italian immigration had increased greatly from the 1890s, but the number of Italian priests had not risen proportionately. In Italy, there was one priest to every 370 people. In America, there was one priest to every 12,000. HJ Desmond wrote, "Catholic Italy, with her rich endowments, her surplus of priests, and her virtual control of the endowments of the Catholic world, should at least look after her own children."[177]

The perceived lack of loyalty to the Catholic faith made the Italians vulnerable to attempts by Protestant leaders to convert the newly arriving immigrants. The Protestants linked conversion with the Americanization of the immigrant because they believed that Protestantism and American democracy were inextricably entwined. The American culture was inherently Christian. Questions arose as to *which* faith, Protestant or Catholic, best exemplified the values of American democracy in the twentieth century. Could Roman Catholics be loyal Americans? Could the Catholic Church, an international organization governed by a titular leader in a foreign country, be an American institution? The Protestants sent gospel wagons and teams of missionaries into immigrant neighborhoods in the 1890s in search of souls to convert. There was street corner and door-to-door proselytizing in the North End. Converts were offered clothing, food and toys, and children were given candy if they attended Protestant services.

In his 1920s biography, Frank Gulinello wrote, "I went home one Sunday and told my father I could not attend children's mass at Sacred Heart

Church because I did not have the nickel necessary for admission. In my time the admission fee in the four Catholic Churches varied according to their 'clientele'—the Irish Church, St. 19s, charged adults 50 cents, Sacred Heart Church, a quarter, and St. Leonard's charged 15 cents." Gulinello cited this incident as the last straw for his family, who then began attending the North End Methodist Church.[178]

Competition between Catholic Churches in Boston

Competition between Catholic churches caused additional issues, such as which parish was permitted to marry the new immigrants at the Boston docks and collect the fees for doing so. For some immigrants, admittance to the United States was predicated on marriage. A woman (and occasionally a man) who arrived to join a prospective spouse was detained by immigration officials until the intended spouse could be notified. It was possible for a justice of the peace to officiate. However, Boston's inspectors preferred that clergy perform the marriage. Under the rules of the archdiocese, only the priest assigned to a given parish could perform marriage and collect the fee unless permission was otherwise pre-obtained by the chancery. At the docks, priests of ethnic churches believed it was their right to perform marriages of people who would or should become members of their church, even though the docks geographically fell in another parish's territory. This conflict caused rivalries between Italian priests and competing churches.[179]

In 1908, Cardinal O'Connell decreed that the only priests who were to have access to the immigrants at the waterfront dock were select members of the North End's two mission orders, the Franciscans and the Scalabrinians. One priest from each order would be designated as the ship greeter, and the two priests would alternate weekly. Cardinal O'Connell ordered, "No other priest has the right to wait on the immigrants or to minister to them or to administer to them the Sacraments." In doing this, he cut out two East Boston churches that had territorial rights to the docks.[180]

Parochial schools were established, but the Italian immigrant peasants did not understand why they had to pay to send their children to school when public schooling was available and free.

The Catholic Charitable Bureau (CCB) was one of the agencies responsible for protecting the Italian immigrant from the proselytizing forces that infested the North End. The bureau formed Sunday School associations in Boston to teach children the catechism along with American patriotism and American loyalty to the church. Copying the Protestants, the Catholics gave gifts to the children who attended classes, while social centers with billiard and reading rooms, singing and dancing clubs, employment bureaus and health clinics were used to attract the young adults.

INTERVENTION BY THE CATHOLIC CHURCH IN ITALY AND INVOLVEMENT OF THE SCALABRINIANS

Meanwhile, in Italy, the Catholic Church feared that the massive migration was going to lead to the loss of immigrant Catholics to Protestantism. Giovanni Battista Scalabrini, the bishop of Piacenza in Italy, was given the task of instituting a congregation that would prepare missionaries to assist immigrants in America.[181] In 1880, Bishop Scalabrini was struck when he saw a group of poor emigrants in the Milan train station ready to leave for the Americas. In 1905, a few months before his death, he proposed the creation of a Central Commission for all migrants, which many consider the precursor of the Pontifical Council for the Dicastery for the Promotion of Integral Human Development. "We Scalibrinians have a bit of that 'suitcase spirit'—the fact that we move our tent to wherever there is a need. The migrants we work with perceive it. They see that we just don't go home at a certain time. They feel we are their companions and they rely on us."[182]

He was supported by Mother Francesco Saverio Cabrini, the founder of the Missionary Sisters of the Sacred Heart of Jesus. The Scalabrinian missionaries opened churches, schools, orphanages and hospitals in America in which Italian was the spoken language.

"Before your Priests came, we believed the Italians were no better off than animals, refractorily to whatever preachment of good, and those abandoned them to themselves," the archbishop of Cincinnati told Scalabrini in 1901. "Today we must admit that the Italian colony is better than all the others."[183]

The Italian religious orders were thought to be more successful than secular priests in attracting and holding the immigrants. This was attributed to their more vigorous defense of their right to provide spiritual care for their countrymen against the pretense of the American clergy.

In a letter dated April 24, 1904, from Father Zabogolio to Bishop Scalabrini, in an attempt to make a general provision for the religious assistance of Italian emigrants, he wrote:

> *Hundreds of thousands of Catholics move every year from Europe, Asia, and Canada to Catholic countries such as Latin America or to Protestant countries like the United States of America and Australia, to live there permanently for many years. Often the local clergy is hardly sufficient for the natives, and because of the differences of language and other reasons, they can do very little or nothing for the immigrants.*
>
> *It is true that those who migrate to Catholic countries remain generally such in name. It is equally true that those who move into protestant countries they themselves, or together with their descendants or the latter ones, lose their faith. The United States, among others is an example. While the progress made by Catholicism is well known and publicized, little known is the enormous loss of faith suffered in the past and continually experienced among emigrants, even those who are thought to be more strongly rooted in it, such as the Irish. There exist statistics, approximate at least, of such losses, but they are little known as no one speaks of them.*
>
> *One must add that a great part of those who have lived for a number of years in the emigration countries and are returning to their hometowns are the cause of ruin of parishes, either because of their laxity of morals or false ideas, or because of their loss or weakening of faith.*
>
> *And if this holds true for many of those who emigrate to and live several years in foreign lands, it is also the case of the very many who go there periodically for some months of the year. They return to infect their towns after scandalizing the people around whom they lived, causing Protestants and schismatics to confirm their prejudice against the Catholic religion and contributing to delaying the day when the nations will form one-fold under one shepherd.*
>
> *To remedy these and other evils of the ever-increasing emigration, something has been and is being done here and there, both in the countries of emigration and immigration. But what is this little when compared to the needs!? Moreover, while nothing was done for people of certain nations and languages, nothing or next to nothing has been done for others (for certain oriental nationalities for example).*
>
> *In order to provide as much as humanly possible, with energy, urgency there should exist in Rome, the center of Christianity, custodian of faith,*

a general office (an "ad hoc" Congregation, or at least a special section attached to a Congregation) with the particular task of preserving the faith of emigrants of any language or nation, both in places of departure and arrival, urging, advising, guiding Bishops, religious and diocesan priests, and the faithful to move to the rescue, providing means and supervision.

This office should, first of all, gather all information as exact as possible on the state of emigration by means of statistics and other publications and with the cooperation of the Bishops of the nations of departure and arrival of emigrants in order to find out how many people of every nation and language migrate to a foreign country, what the causes of their total loss or partial loss of faith and good morals, whether any provisions have been taken yet, and if so which ones. Then it should urge the Bishops themselves to discuss with their clergy in diocesan and in regional, provincial, and national meetings and find means and ways to eventually be adapted in accord with the directives of the Congregation in charge within the Holy See.

Since the lack of qualified workers of the Gospel as to language, customs, and the different temperaments of the various nationalities is the proximate cause of the lamented evils, the Congregation in charge could, whenever needed, promote the funding of seminaries specifically for the different languages or nations, or of Congregations like the one founded by Bishop Scalabrini of Piaceza (for emigrants of Italian language) and interest the Superiors of various religious orders and congregations in sending missionaries wherever the need would be greater. To places where it should not be possible to send diocesan or religious priests as resident missionaries, care should be taken at least that there be priests who would periodically go wherever the different groups of emigrants may be, so that these unfortunate ones will be allowed to enjoy the comfort of experiencing at least an occasional presence of God's messengers.

To obviate to the so-often lamented evils brought about by both temporary and permanent migration, the central office or Congregation in Rome could adopt these and other provisions, which an accurate study of the state and conditions of emigration and the advice of Bishops and other people well known for their piety should suggest.

Emigration does not show signs of decrease; rather considering the populations increase and modern means of communication that are evermore multiplying and making progress, it will continue to increase.

Already distances no longer exist. In olden days emigration was generally contained within the confines of a certain nation or the neighboring ones.

Nowadays it is easier to travel to America than it was about half a century ago to move from many towns of Lombardy (as it was then the practice) to Palermo, Naples, Rome or even to Venice or Genoa.

Should there be a small decrease in emigration in one nation there will be another one to take its place; the Catholic nations will contribute greater contingents to emigration....It is my humble opinion that from these considerations the conclusion should be drawn that besides providing a remedy for such great evils, the institution of a central office charged with directing and coordinating the assistance of emigrants spoken of above would bring great benefits.

In essence the enemy in the United States is Protestantism, hard at work at perverting Catholic souls. Outlined practical solutions, such as founding parishes for each nationality found, Italian parishes where population is mixed and clergy is mixed should serve; priests should be possibly the same nationality as the parishioners or at least know the language and let there be in every parish in the US a school where together with English and elementary instruction the national language of the parishioners be taught.[184]

He concluded with his suggestion that the Holy See should arrange for the congregation to oversee this. And they did. As we will see in the next chapter, the Scalabrinian fathers rolled up their sleeves and were instrumental in bringing peace to the growing friction bubbling up in the North End among the Italian factions.

The relationship between the Italian immigrant, the Catholic Church, the Catholic Church in America and America itself is a complicated one that has evolved over time.

6

EVOLUTION OF TWO NORTH END CHURCHES

There was little unity among Catholics in the North End. There was friction between the Irish Catholics and the Italian Catholics, and the Italian Catholic community itself was divided by regional origins.

Seeing the need for a church that catered to the Italian immigrant, in 1873 Archbishop Williams called on the Italian Franciscans, many of whom were themselves Italian immigrants, to begin the process of establishing such a church. The Italian Franciscan friars had first come to America in 1855, settling in New York and then moving on to Pennsylvania, Connecticut, Texas and Lawrence, Massachusetts, before they arrived in the North End.

ST. LEONARD OF PORT MAURICE CHURCH

Saint Leonard of Port Maurice Church (founded by Father Angelo Conterno, OFM, later joined by Father Joseph Guerrini) became the first Catholic Church established for Italians in the North End and the second or third in the country for the religious and spiritual care of Italian immigrants. It was established one hundred years after the founding of Old North Church.[185]

The church was built on a small lot known as the Hooten Estate lot on Prince Street that had been purchased for $9,000. Within a decade, the continued influx of Italian immigrants made it clear a larger space was needed, and by the mid-1890s, the parishioners numbered close to twenty thousand.

Father Ubaldus Pandolfi, OFM, working with the community, raised $160,000 (the equivalent of more than $4 million today), and a new, larger church was built. The parish was thriving—perhaps too well.

Most of the North End immigrants were Genoese who strongly resisted the Irish Catholic structure, and the archdiocese understood the importance of having an Italian church in the North End. The work was difficult. Father Guerrini was the first priest specifically designated to care for the Italian community of the Boston archdiocese. This included the Italian Catholics in Boston proper and an additional two thousand Italian Catholics in the one thousand square miles around Boston. There was a mandate. Even if the parish was Italian, confessions had to be in English. The archbishop hoped to encourage the Italian Catholic community to become bilingual. The Genoese Italians attending St. Leonard's became resentful and protested that the church, which was supposed to be for the use of Italians, was being frequented by the Irish in great numbers.[186]

The parishioners also complained that the church was catering to the Irish parishioners and believed the funds at St Leonard's were being mismanaged. Franciscan Father Guerrini was a popular pastor but a

St. Leonard's of Port Maurice Church. *Boston Public Library*.

St. Leonard's of Port Maurice Church. *Boston Public Library.*

poor administrator. He was unable to raise adequate funds to meet the annual costs of maintaining the parish. Creditors obtained a warrant for his arrest after finding that the financial condition was so serious that the church was $30,000 in debt. In 1878, Father Guerrini went to New York rather than face his creditors. He was sent back to Italy in December, left the Franciscan order the following year and went to Australia as a missionary priest.

Father Boniface Bragatini was sent in to replace Father Guerrini as pastor of St. Leonard's and to settle the financial situation. His administration of the church (1878–87) was even more turbulent than that of Father Guerrini. The Irish continued to use St. Leonard's. Greatly upset by the catering to the Irish and the financial difficulties of St. Leonard's, the Genoese formed a society called the Societa Cattolica Italiana to formalize plans to either buy the abandoned Protestant Seamans Bethel Chapel in North Square or erect a new structure in the North End.[187]

San Marco Society and Purchase of Seaman's Bethel Chapel

Early in 1884, a delegation from Societa Cattolica Italiana formed the San Marco Society, collected money on its own and purchased the abandoned nondenominational Protestant Seaman's Bethel Chapel in North Square.[188]

The Genoese wanted a say in the administration of the church similar to the *fabbriceria* in Italy in which they would control the real estate. In America, this concept became to be known as "trusteeism" and took various forms.

In its most moderate form, it sought to assert the right of the laity, through their representatives or trustees, to participate in the management of the financial or other temporal affairs of the church, that they had the right of *jus patronatus*—to choose their own pastors and dismiss them. The American Catholic Church thought it unwise for laity to participate in the government of the church.

The San Marco Society discussed this possible purchase with Father Bragantini. He agreed a new church was needed and suggested that the purchase of the Bethel Chapel would be more economical than building a new structure. Members of the San Marco Society insisted that the church be structured in accordance with the fabbriceria system they had been familiar with in Italy. Father Bragantini did not agree because it would be contrary to local practice and would give the Genoese greater control in an already fracturing Italian Catholic community. There was also concern that laity would challenge church hierarchy, control the parish priest or defy the bishop.

Controversy within a congregation or between a priest and bishop threatened the church because it attracted scandal.

San Marco Society and Conflict with the Archdiocese of Boston

The Genoese purchased the property for $28,000 ($10,000 cash and a mortgage of $18,000) without the permission of the diocese. The $10,000 was raised in one month. This was a violation of church law. The congregants asked the archdiocese for a priest. The Boston Archdiocese refused their request, siding with Father Bragantini. Archbishop Williams had a high regard for the Franciscans but regarded the San Marco Society members as malcontents, rebels against legitimate authority and champions of the dangerous trustee system. He was firmly determined not to allow the chapel to be used as a church unless title to it and all other churches were transferred to him unconditionally.[189]

One commentator, Anna Martellone, wondered at the time whether Archbishhop Williams's denial of the right to consecrate the church was based on the advice of some opponents worried about the possible transgressive spirit of the San Marco Society or whether it was just a manifestation of the difficult relationship between the Irish Catholic hierarchy in Boston and the Italian immigrants.[190]

The San Marco Society refused to transfer the title, convinced that they were defending their rights as laity. This began six years of litigation in Rome between the Genoese and the Franciscans. During that time, the society members attended Mass at English-speaking churches but for all devotions gathered at the chapel, where laymen received and spoke of the Gospel and led in recitation of the rosary and other traditions. The San Marco Society sent Tommy Brichetto as emissary to the Vatican to obtain the necessary documents to proceed following the hierarchical lines.[191]

In a letter, Cardinal Simeoni wrote (translated from Italian):

> *I do not know if your Eminence knows that in Boston there is a congregation of Italians, having their own church, who do not want to relate to the local clergy. I do not know for what reason. These poor people, several thousand, for every feast gather at the church, singing the Kirie, the Gloria, the Credo, etc. and reciting the Rosary. They come back in the evening for Vespers and the Second Rosary, always without a priest. They do not want to use the churches indicated by the Archbishop. Therefore, after the continuous suggestion of the settlers, I thought to send there F. Zaboglio, General Secretary of our Congregation to see if and how it would be possible to solve this disorder. I hope, if the Archbishop will agree, that I will quickly send two missionaries and some catechists, but I will write to you about it another time.[192]*

The letter highlights two fundamental points in the evolution of Italian assistance in the United States. First, the fear of transgressive, even heretical, behavior and second, the attention of the newly organized Scalabrini fathers devoted to the problems of the immigrants.

On July 20, 1888, Father Frances Zaboglio, priest of the Pious Society of the Missionaries of St. Charles, came to Boston to intercede on behalf of the San Marco Society. The archbishop took a hard line, demanding that the building in North Square be closed and that no more religious services be held there. He demanded it remain closed until title to the church was transferred to him. The archbishop did acknowledge that a second place of worship was needed for the Italian Catholics in the North End, as St. Leonard's had become much too crowded. He allowed Father Zaboglio to seek a venue as long as it was not the North Square edifice.

Father Zaboglio rented a hall at 86 Beverly Street, and on December 23, 1888, he opened a chapel. For a year and half, the congregation worshipped there.

The San Marco Society worked through those they knew in Italy to lobby for a decision from Rome in their favor. In February 1889, Bishop Francesco Satolli was sent by Pope Leo XIII on a tour of the Italian missions in North America, partly in response to the failures of the 1884 Third Plenary Council of Baltimore to address how Italian Catholics could be better cared for. When he visited the dilapidated Beverly Street Chapel the San Marco Society had been allowed to use for several years for Masses, he was appalled and described it to Pope Leo as a "cave."

Negotiations in Rome

Because of his visit and his comments to the pope, a new round of negotiations opened up in February 1890. Three months later, Archbishop Williams agreed that St. Mark's Church could be opened for worship. The Scalabrini Fathers were appointed as overseers. On May 25, 1890, Father Zaboglio consecrated the church. The controversy was finally concluded, thanks to the mediation of Father Francesco Zabaglio. Legal restrictions remain on the deed today.

In an oral interview with William DeMarco in 1979, Joseph Tassinari, then president of the San Marco Society, said:

The archbishop was stubborn, but we won in the long run. What eventually happened was that the property in North Square—both the church and rectory—remained in the name of the Saint Mark Society. The archbishop had the legal right to take the property from us at his discretion provided, if—and this is a big IF—we agreed, either with the price or the acceptance of the alternate site he wanted to provide us with. To my knowledge we

*are the only lay organization in the US to legally own a Catholic Church,
even today. We also won on the Franciscan issue. The archbishop allowed
us to keep the Scalabrini Fathers. The church is still run by the fabbriceria
system, because all financial matters must meet with my approval and that
of the executive board. We are also unique in that situation. One thing
Archbishop Williams did win out on was that we could not use the church
if we did not change the name. I guess the name "Saint Mark's Church"
must have given him some sleepless nights. The society agreed upon the
name Sacred Heart Italian Church in 1890.*[193]

ARCHDIOCESE ATTEMPT TO CLOSE SACRED HEART CHURCH

And so, there were two Italian Catholic churches in the North End in
proximity to each other: St. Leonard's of Port Maurice and Sacred Heart
Church. Each church attracted Italians from specific villages within similar
Italian provinces. It was unthinkable for the members of one church to
attend Mass in the other Italian church. A parishioner would rather attend
an Irish Catholic church nearby than attend the "wrong" Italian church.

In 2003, the Scalabrinian local province made a decision to remove
priests from Sacred Heart Church if the archdiocese requested them to
do so in order to relocate their increasingly scarce resources to geographic
areas that had more evident needs for their Italian immigrant parishioners.
They considered the mission they began in the 1880s to assist the Italian
immigrants in the North End accomplished.

In 2003, the archdiocese announced a plan to close Sacred Heart Church.
Two hundred parishioners who did not want the church closed attended two
protest meetings. Members of the San Marco Society Bennett and Richard
Molinari protested and wrote an article in the North End newspaper, the
Post-Gazette, on April 2, 2004, making a point that the North Enders claimed
ethnic privilege. The church was supposed to benefit Italians. They did not
feel the Catholic hierarchy recognized ethnic privilege.[194]

According to scholar Frederick Barth, boundaries are important in
maintaining the continuity of ethnic groups. The issues surrounding the
closure of Sacred Heart Church demonstrated this dynamic. Sacred Heart
was a boundary marker that was both social and territorial. It was not
just a neighborhood parish. It had also become a symbol of an Italian

community and not just within the geographic neighborhood of the North End. It was also a symbol for the Italians who had left the North End and moved to the suburbs.[195]

All the North End societies participated in the protest, sharing their concern about what they perceived as an attack on Italian identity. To the protestors, closing Sacred Heart implied the acceptance of a decision taken in a different place by different people. It also presupposed the acceptance of that decision—that there were no longer enough Italian immigrants in the North End (as declared by the Scalabrinians) and that there was thus no longer the need for an official Italian church, since the archdiocese had made a decision to preserve the Franciscan St. Leonard's, which was no longer considered a church just for Italians.

The Molinaris and their protestors were aware that there was also a risk to the school connected to the church; people could lose their jobs, and Sacred Heart was the target of a complex maneuvering about lucrative real estate. The protestors and the San Marco Society felt excluded from a decision about something they felt belonged to them. To them, Sacred Heart was owned by the San Marco Society and given in trust to the archdiocese.

On September 1, 2004, the Sacred Heart Parish was closed as an official parish of the Archdiocese of Boston. Archbishop Sean O'Malley (a Franciscan friar) approved the closing, stating, "The Italians no longer live here. They are no longer the humble peasants destined for the mills in Lawrence or Lowell, employed to dig the local subway, receive starvation wages. It is necessary to pay attention to the needs of the new immigrants that have arrived in the city."

Archbishop O'Malley underscored the three reasons for his reconfiguration project: first, there was a change in demographics. The trend characterized by building churches and opening parishes to accommodate immigrants from overseas was now outdated. Neighborhoods had changed, as past immigrants moved to the suburbs and new immigrants moved into the city. Second, there was a decline in clergy, and third, many other parishes had overwhelming economic problems.

In 2005, the trust was upheld in civil court in Boston. The Archdiocese of Boston was represented by the Boston law firm Rogers and Rogers. The San Marco Society retained its own counsel both in Boston and in Rome. Once again, the trust was upheld at the Apostolic Signatura in Rome, the Catholic Church's equivalent of the Supreme Court. And so, the suppression of the Sacred Heart Parish was allowed by the archdiocese, but the trust was acknowledged and found to be in perpetuity.

Today the church remains empty and intact. The restrictions in the deed mattered. The archdiocese did not have the unilateral right to close the church and sell the property. There are plans in place to perhaps turn it into a Franciscan Center.

ROLE OF FRANCISCAN FATHERS IN NORTH END CHURCHES TODAY

Today the Franciscan Fathers are responsible for the three Catholic Churches in the North End: St. Leonard's of Port Maurice, St. Stephens and the Sacred Heart Church. Two of them, St. Leonard's and St. Stephens,[196] are open and active. In addition to their direct religious activities, the churches have stepped in and provided substantial community assistance. St. Leonard's and the Franciscans built St. Anthony's School, which gave many priests, brothers, sisters and public servants to the local community. In 1907, when it was completed, the Franciscan Sisters of the Immaculate Conception took over the education of the immigrant children. The 1917–19 Spanish flu left many Italian orphans. The then pastor of St. Leonard's, Father Anthony Sousa, OFM, founded the Home for Italian Children in Jamaica Plain. During the U.S. bicentennial, St. Leonard's built its beautiful Peace Garden. In 2023, St. Leonard's celebrated its 150th anniversary.

Sacred Heart Church is closed for now, but directions for its future are being explored.

7
FEASTS

When the Italians settled in the North End, they brought with them traditions of the villages and provinces they had left in Italy. One of the most important was that of the feasts.

Each village in Italy had a patron saint. Worship of saints was a fundamental part of Italian Catholicism, but it was different from the formal practices of the Catholic Church. Saints were intermediaries in the people's transactions with God, who was supreme and divine. The feasts of the saints were part of the religion of the streets, not of the church, and, as a result, were not without controversy.

AMERICAN CATHOLIC VIEW OF THE ITALIAN FEASTS AND SOCIETIES

The concept of a feast with patron saints was foreign in America. Americans, Catholics (particularly Irish Catholics) and Protestants regarded the Italian immigrants as little better than pagans and idolaters. Protestant missionaries thought them "just as ignorant of the true Christ and Christian way as any heathen in the darkest Africa" and considered the feasts "nothing more than sensual orgies with music and fireworks."

Even some Italian clergymen found the way the feasts were celebrated in America objectionable. They claimed the proceeds of the feasts flowed

North End feast. *Vito Aluia collection.*

into the coffers of the societies or the promoters rather than the church. Don Luigi Guanela asserted that "these sacred, profane feasts, where the profit motive is mixed with that of material entertainment should be prohibited."[197]

Condemnation from every quarter, however, appeared to have little effect upon the immigrants. When the church did prohibit feasts, the societies proceeded to hold them without the benefit of clergy or even with the services of defrocked priests.[198]

Giacomo Gambera, an Italian priest, wrote in his autobiography,

> *First of all, in a city in which you have a mixture of nonbelievers and those of other faiths, the parading of statues exposed religion to irreverence and derision. In the second place, the promoters of these external feasts were generally not trustworthy individuals. They were not exemplary. They were not practicing Catholics and they were suspected of pure speculation. In fact, without any authorization they used to solicit offerings from their fellow townsmen in the name of the feast of the parish. Then when the parade was over, they would strip the statue of the offerings made and not render an account to the society.[199]*

Whatever the objections associated with them, however, the observance of feast days was too deeply ingrained in the southern Italian culture to be easily eradicated and continues today.

Italian Feasts in the North End

In the North End, there are different Italian American feasts, or festivals, dedicated to the various Catholic saints who are the patrons of different Italian villages. The feasts are organized by laymen. Each patron saint has a society (a voluntary association) in the name of the patron saint. The societies were (and still are) places for Italian immigrants to get together and socialize with those of their villages. The societies have secular activities, such as guest speakers, bingo, coffee. Association with a society is voluntary, exclusionary and geographically based. It is a collection of individuals who gather together for moral and social reasons in the name of their patron saint. There is little relationship between the churches in the North End and the feasts. Societies are not part of the church. They are self-proclaimed religious societies carrying the name of the saint.[200]

Most important is the connection between the old world and the new. One of the main characteristics of religious festivities is the evident ability to generate what sociologist Emile Durkheim defines as the "collective effervescences" of emotions and social energy, the fundamental elements that strengthen the social bonds between ritual participants and create confusion at a structural level. Seeing religion as "something eminently social," Durkheim argues that through its rites, religion acts as a source of solidarity, identification and cohesion and provides occasions for people to gather and reaffirm their social norms. It is precisely during rituals that men who feel "united in part by blood ties but even more by a community of interests and traditions" gathered and became conscious of their moral unity. In particular, during ritual actions, dominant symbols (such as the statue or effigy of the patron saint) bring the ethical norms and values of the social group "into closer contact with strong emotional stimuli."[201]

The Patron Saint

From this perspective, the celebrations to honor local patron saints (throughout Sicily) can be interpreted as an occasion for the community to maintain and reaffirm its collective life, historical narrative, shared emotions and dominant ideas at periodic intervals.[202]

Similarly, the statue of the patron saint carried in procession through the streets of the towns represents the "sacred" object for the extended community, its "totem," for it is set apart and different from all other "profane things." In other words, religious symbols represent the group, and the worship of these symbols by the group reproduces its existence. This has significant implications for the stability and social structure of society.[203]

The potential of a ritual performance to strengthen the social bonds between individuals—and between individuals and the social context of the ritual itself—may also have important implications for the power and authority of the leaders conducting it. In order to preserve their social power and the ability to exercise control, leaders of social groups (or elites) need to "develop effective forms of expressive communication" and transform their "interest conflicts" into widely available performances that project symbolic forms. Therefore, the goal of the ritual as performance, whether on stage or in society, remains the same as the ambition of sacred ritual. They stand or fall on their ability to produce psychological identification and cultural extension. The aim is to create, via skillful and affecting performance, the emotional connection of the audience with actor and text and thereby generate the conditions for projecting cultural meaning from performance to audience.[204]

NORTH END FEAST SOCIETIES

In the North End, the largest feast is the Feast of St. Anthony of Padua of Montefalcione, which has been celebrated in the North End since 1919, when a group of Italians from Montefalcione settled there. The main event is a ten-hour procession carrying the statue of St. Anthony through the North End streets.

The Fisherman's Feast is also noteworthy. Its patron saint is Madonna del Soccoros, or our Lady of Help, the patron saint of Sciacca, Sicily. She has protected the citizens of Sciacca since the fourteenth century. Fishermen have a special relationship with her, as they brought the heavy marble statue into the Sciacca port in the early sixteenth century. In the North End, her statue is brought each year to Boston Harbor to bless the fishing grounds. The climax of the Fisherman's Feast is the flight of the angel. Three young girls are chosen to play angels. One girl is the main angel, and the other two are supporting angels. From a balcony high above the crowd, the two supporting angels recite prayers. The main angel emerges from a window and "flies" above the crowd, landing in front of the statue to pray. As she begins her return flight to the window the crowd roars and confetti is thrown.

In the early days, membership in a society was highly selective. The only way to become a member of the Society of St. Anthony of Padua of Montefalcione, for example, was to be born in Montefalcione. As new generations came to be, this relaxed and became membership by degrees of kindred.

An example of the connection between the villages in Italy and the North End is found with the Society of the Madonna Della Cava (located on Battery Street). The villagers from Pietraperzia congregated mostly on Battery, Charter and Hanover Streets and Salutation Alley. They brought with them their faith in Madonna Della Cava and her celebration. The feast of Madonna Della Cava is the second week of each August and coincides with the festival held in Pietraperzia, Sicily. The miracle of Madonna Della Cava began in Italy. In the early thirteenth century in the village of Trapani, in the northwest corner of Sicily, lived a young mute boy. He had lost his ability to speak at birth. One night, Madonna Della Cava visited him in a dream. She said to him: "Come in and uncover me from the ground." Madonna told the young boy where she lay buried, in the nearby town of Ronzi in the central province of Enna. The next morning, the boy awoke and tried to tell his mother about his dream. But the mother dismissed his story, thinking it to be only his imagination. Madonna visited the boy in a second dream and asked him to uncover her. A second time, the boy told his mother about the dream and the mother ignored him. Finally, the Madonna visited the boy in a dream for a third time. She implored him to uncover her from the earth. This time, the boy pleaded so strenuously with his mother that she became convinced there may be merit to his dream. Hence, the mother, son and other villagers who were equally impressed with the story of the young boy's dreams traveled to the town of Ronzi. There they began to dig in one area. They did not find Madonna, so they erected a shrine on the site of this digging in her honor. Then they again began digging in a second spot, all to no avail. They erected still another shrine on the spot of this second excavation. On the third effort, the people found their reward. In the ground lay an enormous, beautifully shining stone with the image of Madonna Della Cava printed on it. The villagers knelt and humbled themselves before this image of Madonna Della Cava. Suddenly, the little boy's speech was miraculously restored. This is the miracle of Madonna Della Cava. The villagers of Trapani tried carrying this stone back to their town. In attempting to do this, the stone fell to the ground and cracked. They interpreted this as a sign that Madonna belonged where she was uncovered. So, they built a beautiful shrine on the spot where Madonna was originally found. This became the Madonna Della Cava Church, which still stands today. The stone bearing the image of the Madonna rests inside the church near the main altar. Pope Inocencia XIII declared via Papal Doctrine the church to be a true parish. The town of Ronzi was renamed Pietraperzia—*pietra* meaning "stone" and *perzia* meaning "town." The natives of this town still worship the Madonna Della Cava, and that tradition continues in the North End today.[205]

In the North End today, other patron saints are Santa Maria DiAnzano, Saint Padre Pio, Madre Pio, Madonna Delle Grazie, San Rocco, St. Joseph, St. Agrippina di Mineo, St. Lucy (Santa Lucia) and Santa Rosalia di Palermo. Today one can be a member of more than one society.

THE RITUAL OF THE FEAST

The laymen who organize the feasts do the planning. There is a feast committee that handles the sponsors, vendors and entertainment. The feasts can range from one day to three days. There is a seven-step process entailed with the ritual of the feast of a society:

THE STATUE OF THE saint is prepared for the ritual. Members of the society enter the chapel in which the statue of the saint resides and prepare the statue to go outside to meet the faithful.

The statue of the saint is carried out and placed on a temporary platform—sometimes with fireworks and gold confetti.

The statue is blessed by a religious figure. In most cases, this is the only role the church takes in the festival, although sometimes in a three-day festival, a Sunday Mass may be celebrated for the saint.

Political leaders pay homage to the saint.

Members near the statue go on duty. The leader (usually the president of the society) and members put ribbons on the statue. Later, dollar bills are attached to the ribbons. The ribbons are held almost exclusively by women (and sometimes children). Other women and sometimes men will bring baskets with religious images and give those images to people who give money to be pinned on the ribbon. The statue is set, and the procession is ready to begin.

The procession starts with the police, then flags (Italian, American and sometimes the Vatican). The president of the society then orders the men under the platform to lift the statue, usually two men in front and one in back to provide balance during the walk. Generally, only men carry the statue. The only exception is the Feast of St. Lucy, in which the statue is carried by women.

The procession is slow because it stops anytime anyone wants to make a financial offering to pin money on the ribbon. (A brass band plays in many feast processions.)[206]

Feasts today are attended by members of all societies (not just the society sponsoring the feast), North End residents and tourists. Societies communicate but do not, for the most part, interact with each other on any formal level. The societies have worked together toward a formal and common goal on two occasions: fundraising after the September 11, 2001 tragedy and rallying against the closure of the Sacred Heart Church in 2004.

8

GENTRIFICATION AND THE FUTURE OF THE NORTH END

The North End the Italians shaped still has the appearance of being Italian. The restaurants, the coffee shops and the pastry shops are still there and thriving. St. Leonard's of Port Maurice Church is still there with its beautiful Peace Garden. Masses are still said in Italian and in English. But many Italians have left the one hundred acres of the North End, and increasingly, a mix of new residents is moving in. Many non-Italians live in the North End today—often in buildings that are now upscale condominiums.

The North End has had boundary changes since the Italians first immigrated there. It has also made some improvements. The Sumner Tunnel was built in 1931, which physically linked the Italian neighborhoods of East Boston and the North End. Many Italians benefited from the construction project.

The Prado was created in 1933. Architect Arthur Shurcliff laid out the open space surrounded by brick walls and mounted plaques that recount the history of the North End. The Prado was a significant physical improvement to the neighborhood and became a gathering place to congregate, socialize and enjoy card games and entertainment. The Paul Revere equestrian statute was created by sculptor Cyrus Dallin and formally revealed on September 22, 1940.[207]

In the late 1930s, Nathan Straus, a well-known advocate of public housing, suggested the entire West End be cleared and replaced with public housing units. Although no action was taken, the creation of the federal

Men on Prado, 1957. *Vito Aluia collection.*

slum clearance program after World War II led the Boston Planning Board to suggest that the fifty-two acres of the West End along with the North End and the South End was an appropriate location for clearance.[208]

NEW BOSTON

In the 1950s, the term "New Boston" was coined by Mayor John B. Hynes to launch his urban renewal project. His plan was the metamorphosis of a broken-down city into an up-to-date metropolis that attracted admiring visitors, not only from its own region but from other parts of the world as well. "There were just as many, on the other hand, who looked on renewal as an unmitigated disaster, with downtown architectural styles that created antiseptic centers devoid of people, institutionalized housing projects that fostered racism and violence, and with an approach to neighborhood conversion that emphasized real estate values and investment profits at the expense of the working class and poor."[209]

Like so many other Bostonians, Mayor Hynes was distressed by the way the expressway was cutting off the North End and the entire waterfront from the rest of the city but could find no alternative to the transportation problem. He could only content himself with the prospect that short-term losses would lead to long-term gains.[210]

Foster Furcolo was the first Italian American governor of Massachusetts (January 3, 1957–January 5, 1961). Ironically, he was a proponent of

Cross and Giufree Streets. *Boston Athenaeum.*

redevelopment and was influential in Boston's Government Center and Scollay Square renewal projects. He was succeeded by another Italian governor, John Volpe, whose parents moved to the North End in 1906 after arriving on the SS *Canopic*, a White Star liner that brought thousands of Italian immigrants to Boston (including my grandfather Anthony Annino and his siblings in 1907).

CENTRAL ARTERY PROJECT

In the 1950s, the Central Artery, an elevated expressway, was built, chewing up part of the old neighborhood and separating the North End from downtown. The Central Artery Project was developed because urban planners expected that car traffic in the city would reach an unbearable level for the dimensions of Boston streets, which had been built in a different era. This project was first suggested in the 1930s after a three-year extensive traffic survey by the Boston Planning Board in its *Report on a Thoroughfare Plan for Boston*. The vision was for an upper-level roadway to provide for traffic going through the Central District of Boston. The Central Artery concept (which was revolutionary at the time) was delayed because of the Great Depression. It was revived in 1948 but hit many problems that delayed construction. There was the steel strike in April 1952. Then hordes of rats infesting the area necessitated an extermination program. The meat handlers who ran the open market at Haymarket were not willing to move until refrigeration in another location was completed. The Chinese objected to significant land loss in Chinatown, and there were protests by North End residents.[211]

The North End residents voiced the most vehement objections to the Central Artery Project because the expressway was scheduled to destroy more than one hundred dwellings and uproot nine hundred businesses. The projected route would slice off the North End from downtown Boston and isolate it. In the spring of 1950, store owners, restaurateurs and food wholesalers organized "Save Boston Business" to protest. North End residents formed a committee to save the North End. The protests did not work. Construction continued.[212]

The Central Artery was finally completed in 1959. With its completion there was a dramatic change in the nexus between the North End and the central district. The North End, now isolated and cut off by asphalt from the city, was an island unto itself. However, the Central Artery Project was important to the North End Italians for another reason: they were beginning to have political power, and it melded them together to negotiate for their own survival.

THE DESTRUCTION OF THE WEST END: NEIGHBOR TO THE NORTH END

In the 1950s, then mayor John B. Hynes launched one of the most ambitious and controversial renewal projects—the redevelopment and ultimate destruction of the entire West End neighborhood (a multi-ethnic neighborhood that abutted the North End and housed many Italian families). Some 3,200 families were displaced. Scollay Square was also destroyed. The homes of the displaced families in the West End were eventually replaced by Charles River Park, a luxury housing development project. Scollay Square was replaced by a new city hall and federal high-rise buildings.[213]

NORTH END/WATERFRONT URBAN RENEWAL PLAN

The North End hit another identity point in 1964 when the Boston Redevelopment Authority proposed the North End/Waterfront Urban

Renewal Plan. Negotiations ensued. It was difficult to know what to do. In the past, the redevelopment of part of a city meant razing it. "On the waterfront no one quite knew how to proceed," architect Ben Thompson recounted. "It was a period of trying to understand how these waterfronts should be used."[214]

In May 1964, in the course of a public hearing, Frederick Langone jumped to his feet when he heard of the proposal of a new ramp from the Central Artery that would exit in front of the mouths of two East Boston tunnels, run along Cross Street and empty into the already congested Haymarket Square and in the process work an inconvenience on his family's undertaking parlor on Hanover Street. "I am certainly not going to go along with that ramp," he protested loudly and withdrew his support for the entire government center project.[215] His argument threw the entire council meeting in turmoil.

Four weeks later, the Boston City Council gave formal approval to Government Center by a 5–4 vote. Langone agreed with it—possibly mollified by an offer by Edward Logue to Langone's brother Joseph of a desirable new location of his funeral parlor.[216]

Robert Kroin, chief architect of the Boston Redevelopment Authority, described what emerged as a collection of attitudes and objectives about what the waterfront should be for the public, rather than an urban plan with specific rules. "We want to see, smell, and hear the harbor as deeply as possible in the city."[217]

Again, the city tried to take a slice of land from the North End. The first proposed plan included demolishing two full blocks of old brick and limestone buildings at the tip of the North End.

In 1972, independent developers and architects joined North End residents to oppose the existing plan and offered a new plan that preserved threatened buildings, built housing for the elderly, allocated more park space and narrowed the roadway. Negotiations ensued. City Representative Frederick Langone was a key negotiator. He began a fight with Boston's city hall on two fronts: the political arena and the courts. His negotiation with then mayor Kevin White resulted in major benefits to the North End. After a long trial for federal housing subsidies, the land in the North End gained by the Langone negotiations resulted in affordable housing, and in 1975, construction for Christopher Columbus Senior Housing Development began.[218]

The waterfront was taking shape. During the Kevin White era, Boston was revitalized—for tourists. Quincy Market (a marketplace of shops and restaurants) became an overnight success. The North End was suddenly next door to the hottest, newest neighborhood. The affordable housing

A History of Grit, Perseverance & Tradition

communities in the North End Langone had negotiated freed up a lot of apartments. Outsiders started to come to the North End for reasons other than the low rent of the past. Young professionals who wanted to walk to work and who enjoyed the energy of the revitalizing city were willing to pay healthy sums for condominiums. Real estate demand exceeded supply. Rents skyrocketed, and condo conversion became a way for the native North Ender to cash out and move to the suburbs (primarily Revere, Saugus, Everett, Stoneham, Medford, Lynnfield, Wakefield, Wilmington, Woburn, Braintree, Winchester, Scituate and Wellesley).

This was a dramatic way for a city to revitalize, and planners across the country took note. As one North End resident, Peter Petrigno, a teacher who grew up in the North End, said, "The turnaround has become so complete that gentrification, not blight, is now the problem for the North End."[219]

THE BIG DIG

The Central Artery Project had not solved the traffic problems in Boston. In the 1980s, the Big Dig (formally known as the Central Artery/Tunnel Project) was contemplated. The goal was to replace the elevated highway of the Central Artery with an underground expressway and to reconnect neighborhoods that had been separated from the city. In the mid-1980s, federal funds were earmarked for the Big Dig. It took a decade to complete, and during that decade, the tremendous construction project further separated the North End from downtown Boston. In a strange way, the isolation of the North End also made it more exotic. It was a protected enclave and an unusual neighborhood that people enjoyed dining in.

Property values continued to increase. In 2004, the Prince Street condominiums were developed, with the developer offering one- and two-bedroom units at the unheard of price of $400,000 to $1,200,000.

ITALIAN ASSIMILATION AND THE FUTURE OF THE NORTH END

Today the Italians have assimilated. A North End regular notes that in the early 1970s when she walked down Salem Street no one spoke English.

121

Men sat in lawn chairs, and all around were people speaking in Italian. That has changed. It is rare to hear Italian spoken while walking down a North End street. Many non-Italians live in the neighborhood, often in the old buildings that have been renovated into upscale condominiums. The imprint of the Italian immigrants on this northern enclave of Boston has endured despite assimilation, urban renewal, gentrification and the pull of suburban living. The area is fixed in the minds of locals with the "little Italy" moniker, notwithstanding the fact that Italian immigrant families are now a minority in the North End. The North End has, ironically, become an important commercial district for the city of Boston that trades on Italian immigrant culture, traditions and values (family, food and festivals), as well as perceptions (the Mafia). As a place, the North End has become a destination to shop and eat and celebrate for locals and tourists alike.

> *The paradox of the North End seems now clear. The prosperity is intimately connected to a declared ethnicity (the perceived safety and good condition of life of the neighborhood seen as a community Italian-style village.) Therefore ,the North End must keep on being Italian even if the Italians are gone. There is a need for identity, above all, because now identity can be considered a scare resource but is central for the economy of the North End. And every symbol declaring a sort of Italianate must be used to maintain this scarce resource. The North End ought to be an Italian neighborhood in general perception and it is necessary to reinforce stereotypes. This is the North End—an imagined community, a state of mind surrounded by water, a declared gemeinschaft, where identity and authenticity have become economic values and exchange goods.* [220]

Claudia Carroll, who organized and managed the 150th Celebration for St. Leonard's Church, noted that what struck her was the traditions that are deeply rooted in the North End. The dedication to the feasts, St. Leonard's and the civic and religious causes they support is deep and long lasting. That tradition is a glue that will keep the North End Italian and keep its character. Even if people move to the suburbs, they come back for tradition.

A lifelong North Ender, Marilyn Frissora reminisced:

> *I think the North End will continue on as the Italian section of the city. Our neighborhood is very rich in history and continues to attract tourists. The many Italian restaurants and St. Leonard's Church (we always called it St. Anthony's Church), having the Italian Mass and the Italian pastry*

shops and bakeries, all contribute to keeping the neighborhood "Italian." There have been many changes since I was a child. It was so beautiful back then and I miss so many things. The ma and pa little shops, the many meat stores and Italian grocery shops selling all the wonderful cold cuts, olives and Italian items, are now few. But with those changes, the character of the North End remains. The North End has remained residential through time. The buildings, with all new construction inside have remained for the most part the same on the outside as well as the schools that have been converted into condos. It remains basically as it was all these years. The North End has fought hard to keep it a residential neighborhood and I believe will continue to do so. Its abundance of historical history (Paul Revere house, Old North Church, Paul Revere Park, etc.) and ethnic background, I believe will remain. The schools in the neighborhood are a huge factor for the families moving into the neighborhood.

We have four affordable senior housing homes, allowing longtime residents to remain here. I do not think this neighborhood would ever be taken over or become industrial. As you said, the water is a big factor as well. I do believe it will continue to be a high-income area, which is sad for those who grew up here and can no longer afford the rent. Would rent control ever return? I'm not sure about that. I doubt it but then again you never know.

This is what I think about our neighborhood going forward. I have such wonderful memories of the North End. As a child we had so much and we all had so little. The area was packed with children playing in front of their houses, and there was a grocery shop on every street. I remember the five and dime on Hanover Street where we would go to buy a trinket or a pebble ball to play with. Everyone sat out in front of their buildings during the summer and every child had a neighborhood of mothers. We all watched out for one another. It was one big family. All of that has somewhat changed and it will never be like that again. We have lost and gained a lot in our neighborhood as well. St. Mary's Church and St. Mary's School, Christopher Columbus High School, St. Anthony's School and the Michelangelo School gone but offering additional residential space. I was the Director of a low income preschool program for many years. I watched the demographics in our neighborhood change, and there was no longer a need for the program. There were fewer families with low income. The neighborhood continues to grow and families are returning. It remains a strong neighborhood. I wish I could go back in time for one day. How I would appreciate all that we had. I would love to see the horse and buggy

123

Thomas Damigella Sr. talking to John Rosato on street corner, 2006. *Damigella family collection.*

coming up the street filled with watermelons and the man shouting out for people to come down to buy them. To hear the music of a Frosty truck or the excitement of visiting the feast. The smell of gravy (pasta sauce) in the neighborhood on Wednesday nights. It was a great place to be. Times have changed but this is home. The North End. Still a great place to be. A neighborhood like no other. It will always live on.

As the North End evolves and changes, will it remain astute enough to retain what has made it a thriving enclave that protects its Italian American residents and brings Italian Americans in from the suburbs along with residents and tourists to the bakeries, cafés and restaurants? It has retained its culture, appeal and identity as many of the other Little Italys in America have lost their way. Lower Manhattan's Little Italy once spanned fifty city blocks. Today that same Little Italy covers about three blocks of restaurants and cafés. The shrinkage began in the 1960s when a wave of Chinese immigrants came in. Chinatown became larger and larger; gentrification came in, and little by little the Italian section of Lower Manhattan became smaller and smaller.

DISTINCT ADVANTAGES FOR THE NORTH END

Boston's North End has distinct advantages. The iconic two-and-a-half-mile Freedom Trail welcomes more than four million visitors each year. It is a well-planned, easy-to-follow trail that connects sixteen nationally significant historic sites (including Faneuil Hall at the edge of the North End and three sites in the North End: Paul Revere House, Old North Church and Copp's Will Burying Ground). It is easy to stop on the trail for lunch, a drink or coffee and a cannoli.

The North End has physical boundaries. It is an identifiable enclave within a city. It is not just a set of city blocks. On one side, it is bounded by water. Although it is part of the waterfront, there is a clear delineation between the North End and the rest of the waterfront. The Rose Kennedy Greenway protects the enclave from the financial district, yet crossing it and entering the financial district is very easy. The North End is accessible yet unique.

The three Catholic churches in the enclave—St. Leonard's Church, Sacred Heart Church and St. Stephen's Church—are the nucleus and the core of the North End. (Sacred Heart's historic rooted past and hopeful future is continuing to evolve.) The churches continue to serve the Catholic and Italian communities. St. Leonard's current pastor, Father Michael Della Penna, is a native North Ender. Today on a Sunday you can attend Mass in English or attend an Italian service. The Italian service draws back into the North End those whose families left. It is a pull to the most fundamental roots of the Italian immigrants, their perseverance and their aspiration.

Prominent North End Italian businessmen, like Frank DePasquale, are investing in the Italian identity. The restaurants De Pasquale owns and manages in the North End are an important anchor in the community (all excellent and each one unique). His major investment in this community at the highest level draws tourists and residents alike.

Today, as Tom Damigella noted, there are two parallel North Ends: the North End that the tourists (both those who walk the Freedom Trail and those who come in from the suburbs) see and the other North End, the Italian neighborhood that is tight and still exists. Many successful North Enders did not move to the suburbs but stayed here, built businesses and restaurants here and have been instrumental in its current energy and success.

Tom Damigella, president of the North End Historical Society, has plans well underway to establish a North End Museum that will educate tourists and residents on the importance of its history and its opportunities for its future.

The North End's excellence in maintaining its Italian culture and identity is luring the children and grandchildren of generations who left the North End for the suburbs to want to come back and live there. Unfortunately for many of them, they are priced out of the housing market.

There are risks that the North End's perimeter is changing with new hotels being built where residential buildings once stood. The risk of aging families cashing out and real estate developers purchasing the buildings and converting them for other uses exists. Any dramatic change will probably come from development within the enclave.

Walking through the North End today, attending Mass at St. Leonard's in either English or Italian, watching the people every single day standing in line wrapped around the block to buy Italian pastries at the bakeries and witnessing the power of Italian American businessmen such as Frank DePasquale continuing to open and operate world-class Italian restaurants, I believe the North End has a strong chance of protecting its ethnic enclave and its Italian identity.

BOCCONCINI AND CURIOUSITA

Most of this book has focused on the history of the journey of the Italian immigrant from Italy to the North End and the evolution of the North End. There is, of course, much more to the North End. This chapter includes some interesting facts and observations about the North End.

Historic Places

Old North Church. Old North Church (originally Christ Church in the city of Boston) was established when the original King's Chapel, located on the Boston Common, grew too small for the growing number of Anglicans in Boston. Subscriptions for the church began in 1722. The sea captains, merchants and artisans who lived in the North End contributed to the funds to build it. Construction began in April 1723. Before the American Revolution, both Patriots and Tories were members of the church and often sat near each other. Although Paul Revere was not a member of the church, he was a bell ringer beginning at age fifteen. Eight change-ringing bells were installed in Old North's steeple in 1745. Change ringing was a seventeenth-century English style of pulling full circle bells in a repertoire of repeating patterns. The Old North church bells are the oldest in the country and are still rung by pulling the bells after the 11:00 a.m. Sunday

Salem Street at Cross Street, Victor Minghella the one-man band, 1945. *Vito Aluia collection.*

service and on special holidays. Today, members of the MIT Guild of Bellringers ring the bells.

Prior to the American Revolution, Patriots worshipped at Old North next to General Thomas Gage, military governor, and Major John Pitcairn of the royal marines. The silver used in the Communion service was a gift to the church by King George II of England in 1733, ten years after its founding.

Queen Elizabeth II visited Boston as part of the celebrations honoring the U.S. Bicentennial on July 11, 1976. "At the Old North Church last year," she said, "your President (Ford) lit a third lantern dedicated to America's third century of freedom and to renewed faith in the American ideals. May its light never be dimmed." Old North Church celebrated its 300th anniversary in 2023.

The Old North Church is a national landmark. It is on Boston's Freedom Trail and is open to the public. (https://www.oldnorth.com).

COPP'S HILL BURYING GROUND was established in 1659 and is Boston's second-oldest cemetery. Its more than 1,200 marked graves include notable

Bostonians from the colonial era into the 1850s. It is on Boston's Freedom Trail and is listed in the National Register of Historic Places.

Historic Events

Great Brink's Robbery. On January 17, 1950, there was an armed robbery of the Brink's building located at 600 Commercial Street. At the time, it was the largest robbery in the history of the United States: $2.775 million was stolen (roughly $31.3 million today), consisting of $1,218,211.29 in cash and $1,557,183.83 in checks. It was unsolved for six years. Less than $60,000 of the stolen money was ever recovered. It is the subject of four movies: *Six Bridges to Cross* (1955), *Blueprint for Robbery* (1961), *Brinks: The Great Robbery* (1976) and *The Brink's Job* (1978).

Great Molasses Flood. In 1919, the Purity Distilling Company's 2.3-million-gallon molasses storage tank, located at 529 Commercial Street, exploded, bursting open and sending a twenty-five-foot wave of molasses weighing approximately twelve thousand metric tons down Commercial Street toward the waterfront, sweeping away all in its path. The wave killed 21 people, injured 150 and caused more than $100 million worth of damage in today's dollars. The flood resulted in one of the first class action lawsuits in the country, as 119 residents sued the United States Industrial Alcohol Company (which had bought the Purity Distilling Company). After three years of hearings, the company paid $628,000 in damages (more than $9.82 million in today's dollars). For more information, see Stephen Puleo's excellent book, *Dark Tide: The Great Molasses Flood of 1919* (Beacon Press, 2010).

USS *Constitution* (Old Ironsides). In 1797, Old Ironsides launched from Edmund Hartt's shipyard on the site of today's U.S. Coast Guard base (427 Commercial Street). Designed by Joshua Humphrey, it won all forty-two of its battles. Old Ironsides now rests in Charlestown's Navy Yard.

Philanthropic, Religious and Civic

Italian Home for Children. The influenza pandemic of 1918 hit the congested North End hard. Father Antonio Sousa, OFM, pastor of St.

Leonard's Church, launched a crusade through sermons and letters to assist the orphans. In 1919, 42 Italian Americans met at St. Leonard's and formed a board of directors and incorporators to create the Home for Italian Children in Massachusetts. In 1920, they raised the funds and purchased the Gahm Estate in Jamaica Plain, a ten-acre farm with a farmhouse and barn. Franciscan nuns operated the school, which opened in 1921 originally with 30 girls aged four to fourteen residing on the premises. In 1929, boys were admitted. From 1921 to 1968, the home cared for approximately 115 children annually. The home is no longer associated with the church. It is now known as the IHC and serves children with behavioral and family problems in a variety of programs (https// www.italianhome.org).

STREET NAMES

The original three streets in the North End were NORTH STREET (originally known as Fore or Front Street, Anne Street, Fish Street and Ship Street), HANOVER STREET (originally known as Middle Street) and SALEM STREET.

The first named street in Boston was Hull Street in the North End, so named around 1700 by Hannah Hull Sewall after her deceased parents. Before 1700, the population was not large enough to require street names. Soon after the naming of Hull Street, the selectmen agreed to name all of the streets in Boston, and by 1708 they had done it. Only fourteen North End streets and alleys retain their original names.

Three streets in the North End are named for cities north of Boston: SALEM, LYNN and MEDFORD.

Hanover Street was named in 1708 as a gesture of loyalty to the new British royal family—the House of Hanover.

Streets named for religious or clergy include STILLMAN for Samuel Stillman of the First Baptist Church, BALDWIN PLACE for Reverend Thomas Baldwin of Second Baptist Church, THATCHER STREET for Reverend Peter Thatcher of Hanover Street's New North Church and WIGET STREET, named in 1894 for Reverend Bernardin Wiget, pastor of St. Mary's Church on Endicott Street.

Two streets are named for taverns: SUN STREET and SALUTATION STREET.

CHARTER STREET is named for an incident in 1691, when the original Massachusetts charter, which the Crown had recently revoked but the colonials were determined to reinstate, was hidden away in the residence of John Foster at the intersection of what are now Foster and Charter Streets.

ENDICOTT STREET was named for Massachusetts governor James Endicott. The original name of PRINCE STREET was Black Horse Lane. (It was named Prince Street in 1708.)

NOTABLE NORTH END RESIDENTS (AND OCCASIONAL VISITORS)

ENRICO CARUSO. Local legend is that the famous opera singer came to the North End to sample the cuisine in the 1930s. He went to a bank to cash a check and could find no way to prove his identity. The teller insisted on some confirmation that he was indeed Enrico Caruso. After a few minutes, he began to sing "Celeste Aida," and when he was done, there could no doubt that he was indeed Enrico Caruso. The check was cashed.

TONY DEMARCO (born Leonard Liotta), American boxer and World Welterweight Champion. Nicknamed "Boston Bomber" and the "Flame and Fury of Fleet Street," he sold out Boston Garden, breaking attendance records. Tony DeMarco Way is a street in the North End named after him. In October 2012, a statue of DeMarco was unveiled at the corner of Hanover and Cross Streets.

JOHN F. FITZGERALD (father of Rose Kennedy and grandfather of President John F. Kennedy). Mayor of Boston in 1906–8 and 1910–14.

ROSE KENNEDY (mother of President John F. Kennedy). Born at 4 Garden Court, she was baptized at St. Stephen's Church. Her funeral Mass was held there too.

INCREASE MATHER, president of Harvard University (1661–1701) and minister of Old North Church (1661–death). Father of Cotton Mather. Resided initially at the site of the historic Paul Revere Home, then at 342 Hanover Street, Boston.

PAUL REVERE (tradesman, civic leader and patriot). Revere was born in the North End on December 21, 1734. He was educated at North Writing School and learned gold and silversmithing in his father's shop. His primary vocation was as a goldsmith (working in both gold and silver). He was considered a master craftsman. On April 18, 1775, Revere left his home at 19 North Square and began the ride for which he became famous. Henry Wadsworth Longfellow's poem "Paul Revere's Ride," written in 1860 and published in the *Atlantic Monthly* in 1861, transformed his legacy from a local to a national folk hero. His home is a national landmark on Boston's Freedom Trail and open to the public.

SOPHIE TUCKER. The Ziegfield Follies star lived at 22 Salem Street for the first eight years of her life, born Sonya Kalish. Her father had deserted the Russian army and immigrated to Boston, finding work under the name "Charles Abuza." From Boston, they moved to Hartford, Connecticut. Her signature song was "Some of These Days."

NORTH END IN THE MOVIES

The Thomas Crown Affair (1968) with Steve McQueen and Faye Dunaway
National Treasure (2004) with Nicholas Cage
The Town (2010) with Ben Affleck
The Brink's Job (1978) with Peter Falk
The Instigators (not yet released as of this writing) with Matt Damon and Casey Affleck

The actor Leonard Nimoy grew up in the abutting West End of Boston.

UNUSUAL AND INTERESTING PLACES

ALL SAINTS WAY. 4 Battery Street, Boston (located in an alley between 4 and 8 Battery Street). North End resident Peter Baldassari has created a shrine to saints, paying tribute to almost every saint canonized by the Catholic Church. His collection includes photos, statues and prayer cards.

NAZZARO COMMUNITY CENTER. 30 North Bennet Street. The Nazzaro Community Center Bath and Gymnasium (formerly known as the North Bennet Street Public, or North End Bath House) is one of the oldest bathhouses. Many of the North End tenements did not have baths or showers. Residents used public bathhouses such as this one, which opened in 1906. Its architecture was inspired by the Villa Medici in Rome. Welterweight World Champion Tony DeMarco trained here. It was sponsored by "Honey Fitz" Fitzgerald, Rose Kennedy's father. It is now a community center.

Peace Garden at St. Leonard's Church. The Peace Garden was established by the Franciscan Friars in 1976 for the Bicentennial.

Skinny House. 44 Hull Street (near the top of the Copp's Hill burial ground). According to local legend, the narrowest house in Boston was built as a spite house shortly after the American Civil War. Two brothers inherited land from their deceased father. While one brother was serving in the military, the other built a large home, leaving the soldier only a shred of property that he felt certain was too small for his brother to build on. When the soldier brother returned, he found his inheritance had been depleted and built the narrow house to spite his brother, blocking out sunlight and ruining his view. Another local legend is of a different opinion—that a builder erected it to shut off the light and impair the view of a hostile neighbor with whom he had disputes. At its widest point, it is 10.4 feet.

54 Snow Hill Street (near Copp's Burial Ground). Built in 1920, the 420-square-foot single-family home is the tiniest single-family home in the North End. It packs a punch and includes a loft bedroom, full kitchen, full bathroom, full living room and a fireplace.

Notable North End Businesses

Some of the early businesses formed by North End residents remain in existence today:

Dragone Cheese. Giuseppe Dragone founded Dragone Cheese in the North End in 1927. It was the largest maker of Italian cheeses in New England. It moved to Medford, Massachusetts, in 1927 and was family operated until it was sold to Saputo in 1973.

Jordan Marsh Department Store. Eben Jordan and Benjamin Marsh went into business together at 168 Hanover Street in the North End selling dry goods for wholesale. Their partnership resulted in the formation of Jordan Marsh, one of the first department stores in America. Jordan Marsh continued in Boston (in a different location) until 2005. It eventually became part of Macy's Department Stores.

Pastene. Luigi Pastene came to Boston from Italy in 1848 and began selling produce from a pushcart. In the 1870s, his son Pietro joined him. Pastene became a company specializing in selling groceries and imported Italian products. In 1901, they expanded to Fulton Street. Today, Pastene is a national brand with distribution and packing facilities in New York, Montreal, New Haven, Havana, Naples and Imperia, Italy. Pastene is now based in Canton, Massachusetts, and remains a family-owned business.

PRINCE SPAGHETTI. In 1912, three immigrants from southern Italy (Gaetano LaMarca, Giuseppe Seminara and Michele Cantella) started a spaghetti manufacturing company at 92 Prince Street in the North End. It was so successful that in 1917 a seven-story building was constructed on nearby Commercial Street, complete with a railroad track that entered through the back, delivering semolina flour directly to the plant. The company was famous for its TV commercial showing a little boy running through the North End streets with the tagline "Wednesday is Prince Spaghetti Day." Eventually, Prince outgrew its location and moved to Lowell, Massachusetts. In 1987, its owners sold to Borden Inc., and ten years later Borden announced plans to close the Lowell plant. It is now part of TreeHouse Foods Inc. In 1974, the original Prince building at 92 Prince Street was converted to condominiums.

STOP & SHOP. In 1883, Solomon and Jennie Rabinowitz (later Rabb) opened a grocery store at 134 Salem Street. Titled the "Greenie Store," it operated at that location until 1908. It was the beginning of the formation of Stop & Shop, the supermarket chain.

BAKERIES

Living in the North End, I have observed that the lines to the bakeries are around the block 365 days a year. Tourists and residents alike line up for their cannolis and pastries.

BOVA'S BAKERY. Antonio Bova and opened A. Bova & Sons Bakery at 79 Prince Street in 1926. The bakery is now three generations old, open twenty-four hours a day, seven days a week and remains family owned. It was recently featured in *The Instigators*, a movie starring Matt Damon and Casey Affleck (https://bovabakeryboston.net).

CAFFÈ DELLO SPORT. Located at 308 Hanover Street, it is known for its unusual coffees and espressos, sandwiches and pastries. On the screen are European futbol (soccer, calcio) Serie A, La Ligua, Premier League, Championship League and more (https://www.caffedellosport.net).

CAFFÈ VITTORIA. Established in 1926, this was the first Italian café in Boston. Located at 290–96 Hanover Street and filled with vintage espresso machines and coffee makers, it is known for its espressos, martinis and cannolis (https://caffevittoria.com).

Modern Pastry. Established in 1930, Modern Pastry began on Hanover Street. It remains family-owned and at 257 and 263 Hanover Street. Three generations of master chefs and over 150 years of authentic old-world methods and experience produce cakes, cookies, candies, torrone, cannolis and pastries for every day and special occasions (www.modernpastry.com).

Mike's Pastry. Michael Mercogliano founded Mike's Pastry on Hanover Street in 1946. Located at 300 Hanover Street, it serves classic Italian pastries and is known in particular for its lobster tails and cannolis (www.mikespastry.com).

Parziale Italian Bakery. Joseph and Anna Parziale arrived from Naples in 1907 and opened Parziale Bakery at 80 Prince Street. They were the first to introduce pizza to New England. The bakery is still owned by members of the Parziale family (www.parzialebakery.com).

Restaurants

There are more than 100 restaurants, cafés and markets in the North End. My husband and I have eaten in just about every one of them. They are all excellent and different. Below are some of our favorites.

De Pasquale Ventures. Frank DePasquale opened his first restaurant, a tiny neighborhood sandwich shop, Il Panino, in 1987. Today, his North End restaurants (Aqua Pazza, Assagio, Bricco, Bricco Salumeria, Bricco Panetteria, Mare, Quattro, Trattoria Il Panino and Umbria) have won numerous awards. DePasquale was named the Massachusetts Restaurant Association Restaurateur of the Year (2017). The quality of his restaurants' food and service is exceptional. Each of his restaurants is different, and each is excellent in its own unique way. Our favorite is Aqua Pazza. Giovanni Tiberini and his team are exceptional (https://depasqualeventures.com).

Mamma Maria. Located at 3 North Square and set in a nineteenth-century brick row house with five private dining rooms, Mamma Mia is an intimate restaurant focusing on historical and traditional Italian dishes (www.mammamaria.com).

Nando. This relatively new restaurant with excellent modern Italian cuisine is located at 393 Hanover Street at the site of the former Green

Cross Pharmacy. The restaurant is owned and operated by members of the pharmacy, making it a continuous family enterprise location (www.nandonorthendboston.com).

REGINA PIZZERIA. Luigi D'Auria founded the popular pizzeria on Thacher Street in 1926. When it opened, there were only a handful of restaurants in the North End. Many residents could not afford to go out to eat at a restaurant. In the 1940s, it was sold to the Polcari family, who now operate twelve Regina Pizzeria locations and two Polcari's Italian restaurants. The original North End location serves tourists and residents, and Regina Pizzeria is now famous throughout the country.

STREGA. Located at 379 Hanover Street and founded by Nick Varano, Strega features elegant meals of Italian-inspired cuisine, featuring homemade pastas (https://stregabynickvarano.com). Its sister restaurant, Nico's, located at 417 Hanover Street, is equally excellent and a little quieter (www.nicoboston.com).

VINOTECA DI MONICA is located at 141–43 Richmond Street, operated by Chef Jorge Mendoza-Iturralde and his family. The menu applies international techniques and ingredients to traditional recipes. His three hardworking children—Sofia, Veronica and Jorge Jr.—make this restaurant special (www.monicasboston.com).

NOTES

1. Emigration from Italy

Important source materials relied on in this chapter include Stephen Puleo's master's thesis, "From Italy to Boston's North End: Italian Immigration and Settlement, 1890–1910"; Stephen Puleo's book *The Boston Italians: A Story of Pride, Perseverance and Paesani from the Years of the Great Immigration to the Present Day*; and Anthony Riccio's books *Boston's North End: Images and Recollections of an Italian-American Neighborhood* and *Stories, Streets and Saints: Photographs and Oral Histories from Boston's North End.*

1. As Anthony Riccio points out in *Stories, Streets and Saints*, 2, from its inception in 1815, the Kingdom of Two Sicilies had actually been a thriving cultural and economic entity. Prior to the northern invasion in the 1860s, the kingdom's booming steel and iron factories produced the materials to construct the first suspension bridge, railway tunnel and gaslight in Italy and supplied the metals to build the largest merchant fleet in Europe. Textile mills and silk factories proliferated throughout the south, employing over 100,000 women. Unemployment was unknown as was the thought of emigration. According to Riccio, unification caused the south to pay a high price: the closing of schools; the looting of banks and treasuries; the disproportionate raising of taxes on the overburdened poor; the enactment of conscription; the dismantling of its iron, steel and textile industries; the loss of farmers' government-sanctioned land; and the indiscriminate murder and plundering of its people by the Piedmontese army. Using the guise of patriotism and national unity as

a means to justify the colonization of southern Italy for its economic benefit, the Piedmontese government created dire conditions that caused millions to leave southern Italy.

2. Killinger, *History of Italy*, 1.
3. Cinel, *From Italy to San Francisco*, 38.
4. Panunzio, "Arriving in Boston," 70–71.
5. It is interesting to note that after 1900 the attitude changed. Not only had emigration thinned out the population, but it also emptied the villages of young men in good health. Italy's youngest, strongest and hardest-working men were seeking their futures elsewhere, and their families followed.
6. Puleo, "From Italy to Boston's North End," 6. The issue of Italian repatriation and the study of the "birds of passage" are critical to our overall understanding of the Italian immigrant experience in America. These factors help explain the Italians' love of homeland despite excruciating hardships, their commitment to financially assist those left behind in the old country, their desire to settle in closely knit neighborhoods in the United States and their resulting slow social assimilation and economic progress within American society. The temporary nature of much of Italian emigration also offered many Americans an excuse to fan the flames of discrimination against the "birds of passage" from Southern Italy who competed for American jobs.
7. Woods, "Notes on the Italians in Boston," 81.
8. Lawrence, *Not So Long Ago*.
9. Puleo, "From Italy to Boston's North End," 38.
10. Giamatti, "Commentary," 14.

2. Immigration and Its Challenges

Important source materials in this chapter include Stephen Puleo's master's thesis, "From Italy to Boston's North End: Italian Immigration and Settlement, 1890–1910," and Vincent Cannato's comprehensive article "Immigration and the Brahmins: An Influx of Undesirables at the End of the Nineteenth Century Hit Boston Elites Rather Hard."

11. Puleo, "From Italy to Boston's North End," 56.
12. The accident was blamed on the "grave error of judgment" of the captain of the SS *Utopia*, John McKeague, who survived the accident. Captain McKeague was arrested. The British court of inquiry in the Port

of Gibraltar found McKeague guilty "firstly in attempting to enter the anchorage…without having first opened out and ascertained what vessels were there and secondly in attempting to turn his ship across the bows of HMS *Anson.*"

13. Traficante, "Great Arrival and Dawn of Italian America." Also, Riccio notes in *Stories, Streets and Saints*, 37, that in 1922 on the *Marietta* at the Cunard Wharf in East Boston, health inspectors boarded the boat and conducted medical examinations. One of the men, Giuseppe Freni, a young Sicilian, was sent to the East Boston Immigration Station on Marginal Street for a medical examination. The doctors found trachoma in both eyes, and he was sent back to Italy, becoming one of many tragic figures in immigration history. See also the Library of Congress's "Immigration and Relocation in U.S. History," https://www.loc.gov.
14. Puleo, "From Italy to Boston's North End," 57.
15. Ibid., 58.
16. "Chapter 10: The Italian Society," 207. Also, it is interesting to note that the North End was not the main focus of these agencies—most who arrived in New York with the assistance of these agencies went to work in Maine and Canada.
17. Amore, *Italian American Odyssey.*
18. Riccio, *Boston's North End*, 3.
19. Ibid., 60.
20. Ibid., 35.
21. Ibid., 58.
22. "Plan to Wipe Out Immigrant Banks," *Boston Sunday Post*, March 6, 1904.
23. "State Asked to Stop the Padrone System," *Boston Post*, February 18, 1904.
24. "Chapter 10: The Italian Society," 205.
25. Commonwealth of Massachusetts, *Problem of Immigration.*
26. Farmelant, "Trophies of Grace," 69.
27. Carr, *Guide to the United States.*
28. Nancy Verde Barr, in her book *We Called It Macaroni*, notes that as long as the first generation of immigrants dominated the Italian communities numerically, the village-oriented social life about food preferences prevailed, in spite of the U.S. government's rather aggressive attempts to alter the Italians' eating habits. Social workers were sent to Italian American homes to convince the immigrants, according to the prevailing nutritional opinion, that too many vegetables in the diet were not good for a person and that meat should accompany starch at every meal. Italian American cooking found a welcome home in the numerous

restaurants that opened to serve cheap Italian food in a homey setting. The mom-and-pop proprietors were eager to please their public and do as the Americans did. They served meat and starch together so that the entrées came with a side of spaghetti or spaghetti and meatballs arrived in the same dish—practices unheard of in Italy. "Salads began to be served before the meal, an American custom rather than in the Italian fashion of after or with the entrée."

29. Lodge, "Restriction of Immigration," 27–36.
30. Ibid., 31.
31. Ibid.
32. Ibid.
33. Cannato, "Immigration and the Brahmins."
34. Ibid.
35. Ibid.
36. Ibid.
37. Ibid.
38. Ibid.
39. Ibid.
40. Ibid.
41. Puleo, "From Italy to Boston's North End," 12.
42. Ibid., 13.
43. Cannato, "Immigration and the Brahmins."
44. Ibid.
45. Ibid.
46. Ibid.
47. Puleo, "From Italy to Boston's North End," 160.
48. Ibid., 145.
49. Ibid., 80.
50. "Did My Family Really Come 'Legally'? Today's Immigration Laws Created a New Reality," American Immigration Council, https://www.americanimmigrationcouncil.org.
51. Pasto, "Immigrants and Ethnics," 106.
52. Ibid., 118.

3. The North End

Important source materials in this chapter include Stephen Puleo's master's thesis, "From Italy to Boston's North End: Italian Immigration and Settlement, 1890–1910"; William DeMarco's excellent book *Ethnics & Enclaves: Boston's Italian North End*; and Christine Compston, Stephen Senge and Walter McDonald's comprehensive book *Rewarding Work: A History of North Bennet Street School*.

53. See generally, DeMarco, *Ethnics & Enclaves*.

54. Puleo, "From Italy to Boston's North End," 61.

55. Ibid., 68.

56. DeMarco, *Ethnics & Enclaves*, 24.

57. Ibid., 69.

58. Woods, *Americans in Progress*, 83, 86–87.

59. Ibid.

60. Puleo, "From Italy to Boston's North End," 128.

61. Ibid., 126.

62. Due to concern with the high mortality rate and poor living conditions, the City of Boston built the North End Park (1893), North End Beach (1893), Copp's Hill Terraces and Prince Street Playground (1897–1901).

63. DeMarco, *Ethnics & Enclaves*, 42.

64. Langone, *North End*.

65. Puleo, "From Italy to Boston's North End," 172.

66. DeMarco, *Ethnics & Enclaves*, 69.

67. Ibid., 75.

68. Ibid., 76.

69. Ibid.

70. Ibid., 84. It is also interesting to note there were several chocolate factories in the North End area: F.L. Daggett (which had locations throughout the city), Liggett's (candy department in Liggett's drugstore a precursor to Rexall), Schraffts (in nearby Charlestown), Lovell & Covel (which later merged with NECCO) and D'Orlando Chocolates on Portland Street.

71. DeMarco, *Ethnics & Enclaves*, 84.

72. Woods, *Americans in Progress*, 372.

73. Allison, *Short History of Boston*, 59. Pauline Agassiz Shaw was the daughter of Louis Agassiz, considered one of the foremost scientists of the nineteenth century. He was a pioneer in the study of glaciers and led collecting expeditions to the Amazon and Great Lakes regions.

He built the Agassiz Museum at Harvard. After his death, his widow, Elizabeth Agassiz, founded and was the first president of Radcliffe College (1879–1903).

74. The discussion of North Bennet School, its history, founders and contribution to the North End is sourced from *Rewarding Work: A History of North Bennet Street School* by Christine Compston, Stephen Senge and Walter McDonald.

75. See Todisco, *Boston's First Neighborhood*.

76. Whyte, *Street Corner Society*. His observations are summarized in this chapter.

77. Separation between Northern and Southern Italians was encouraged by the Northern Italians, who were embarrassed to be associated with the peasants and farmers from the south. There were two reasons for this: years of north versus south feuding in Italy carried over to life in the United States, and by the time of the great emigration from southern Italy, Northern Italians had begun to establish themselves here. Many had small businesses or were professionals.

78. Todisco, *Boston's First Neighborhood*, 36.

79. Gans, *Urban Villagers*.

80. Ibid., 208.

81. Ibid.

82. Ibid.

83. Ibid.

84. Piccoli, "Italian Immigration in the United States."

85. Todisco, *Boston's First Neighborhood*, 45; *Boston Evening Transcript*, October 5, 1927.

86. Todisco, *Boston's First Neighborhood*, 47.

87. George Robert White, owner of the Potter Drug and Chemical Company, died in 1922. In his Will, he left $5 million to the City of Boston as a permanent charitable fund, the net income of which was to be used only for creating public beauty and utility for the inhabitants of Boston and is not allowed to be used for any of the normally provided services of the city. Money from the fund was used for the commission of the Paul Revere statue in the Prado and for the thirteen memorial plaques installed in the Paul Revere Mall in 1940.

88. Todisco, *Boston's First Neighborhood*, 48.

89. Ibid., 53.

90. Ibid.

91. Pasto, "Immigrants and Ethnics," 111.

92. Ibid., 106.

4. Cultural Cracks in the North End

93. Whyte, "Race Conflicts in the North End," 625. It is interesting to note that his observations are just that—observations. They are not based on science or empirical evidence.
94. Whyte, "Race Conflicts in the North End," 625.
95. Ibid.
96. Ibid.
97. Ibid.
98. Ibid.
99. Ibid.
100. Ibid.
101. Sweeney, *Gangland Boston*, chapter 4.
102. Puleo, *Boston Italians*, 18.
103. Ibid.
104. Ibid.
105. D'Amato, "Black Hand Myth."
106. Ibid.
107. "Charles Ponzi," Wikipedia, https://en.wikipedia.org/wiki/Charles_Ponzi; Darby, "In Ponzi We Trust."
108. Quoted in Riccio, *Stories, Street and Saints*, 59.
109. Herwick, "This Week in History."
110. Allison, *Short History of Boston*, 85–87.
111. Janjevic, "Catholic Church Was 'Inconsistent,'" quoting Rossella Merlino. The relationship between the Catholic Church and the Mafia has been inconsistent. Until the 1980s, the general position of the highest hierarchies of the Catholic Church had been of acquiescence toward and even tolerance of the Mafia; Merlino, "Sicilian Mafia, Patron Saints and Religious Processions." It is interesting to note that Pope Francis excommunicated all Mafiosi on June 22, 2014.
112. Puleo, "From Italy to Boston's North End," 79.
113. Sweeney, *Gangland Boston*, chapter 5.
114. Ibid.
115. Ibid, chapters 7 and 9.
116. Ibid., chapter 16.
117. Ibid., chapter 26.
118. Ibid., chapter 34.
119. "Frank Anguilo's Death Marks End of North End Mob Era," *Boston Globe*, June 1, 2015.

120. Ibid.
121. Ibid.
122. Puleo, *Boston Italians*, 105.
123. Ibid.
124. Ibid.
125. Ibid., 118.
126. Ibid.
127. Watson, *Sacco and Vanzetti*, 64.
128. Boston Public Library Rare Books Department MS 2030, Box 4A Folder 4, Item 7 (Shelf Locator).
129. "Sacco and Vanzetti," Wikipedia, https://en.wikipedia.org/wiki/Sacco_and_Vanzetti.
130. Frankfurter, *Case for Sacco and Vanzetti*.
131. Dos Passos, *Facing the Chair*.
132. Watson, *Sacco and Vanzetti*.
133. Ibid., 345.
134. Ibid., 339.
135. Ibid.
136. Doss Passos, "They Are Dead Now," 228–29.
137. Bullard, "Proposed Reforms Echo"; "Fuller Urges Change in Criminal Appeals," *New York Times*, January 5, 1928.
138. Massachusetts General Laws, 1939, ch. 341.
139. "Sacco and Vanzetti."
140. Ibid.
141. "History of Italian Americans in Boston," *Boston Globe*, March 18, 1891.
142. *Boston Globe*, August 30, 1905.
143. Pope-Obeda, "Expelling the Foreign-Born Menace."
144. Ibid.
145. Federal Bureau of Investigation, fbi.gov.
146. Ibid.
147. Ibid.
148. Pope-Obeda, "This Deportation Business."
149. Puleo, "From Italy to Boston's North End," 200.
150. Gamm, *Urban Exodus*, 75.
151. *Boston Globe*, December 17, 1942.
152. *Boston Globe*, October 18, 1942.
153. Staples, "How Italians Became 'White.'"

5. Italian Americans and the Catholic Church

Important materials for this chapter include Kristen Farmelant's master's thesis, "Trophies of Grace: Religious Conversion and Americanization in Boston's Immigrant Communities"; Rudolph J. Vecoli's article "Prelates and Peasants: Italian Immigrants and the Catholic Church"; William DeMarco's book *Ethnics & Enclaves: Boston's Italian North End* and Mario Francesoni's chapter in volume 4 of the *History of the Scalabrinian Congregation.*

154. Vecoli, "Prelates and Peasants," 221, quoting Howard R. Marraro, *American Opinion on the Unification of Italy 1846–1861*, 241–304.
155. Vecoli, "Prelates and Peasants," 221.
156. Ibid.
157. Ibid., 222.
158. Ibid., 224, quoting *Chicago Times*, October 3, 1870; *New World*, October 7, 1893; September 14, 1895; February 25 and March 4, 1911.
159. Vecoli, "Prelates and Peasants," 222.
160. Ibid., quoting Giovanni Schiavo, *Italian American History*, vol. 2, *The Italian Contribution to the Catholic Church in America.*
161. Vecoli, "Prelates and Peasants," 222.
162. Ibid., 237, quoting Dunne, "Church and the Immigrant," 1–15.
163. Commager, *American Mind*, 193.
164. Browne, "Catholicism in the United States," 103.
165. Without exception, the Italians held the Irish responsible for their grievances. The Italians were convinced the Irish who succored the people with money and men were religious fanatics and sworn enemies of la patria. *L'Unione Italiana*, December 4, 11, 25, 1867.
166. Agnew, "Pastoral Care of Italian Children," 260.
167. Vecoli, "Prelates and Peasants," 222; *Chicago Record-Herald*, February 28, March 1, 1908.
168. Vecoli, "Prelates and Peasants," 223.
169. Ibid., 228.
170. Ibid., 229.
171. Ibid.
172. Ibid., 230, quoting Bernard J. Lynch.
173. DeMarco, *Ethnics & Enclaves*, chapter 4.
174. Ibid.
175. Vecoli, "Prelates and Peasants," 268.

176. Lord and Harrington, *History of the Archdiocese*, 220, quoting Reverend Al Palmierie.
177. Vecoli, "Prelates and Peasants," 246.
178. Gulinello's unpublished biography is quoted in Farmelant, "Trophies of Grace."
179. Farmelant, "Trophies of Grace," 52.
180. Ibid.
181. "Why the Pope Decided St. Scalabrini Didn't Need a 2nd Miracle for Canonization," Aleteia, October 9, 2022, https://aleteia.org. On October 9, 2022, Pope Francis canonized Bishop Scalabrini, who founded missionary orders of men and women in the 1880s to provide for the pastoral needs of large numbers of Italian immigrants. He founded the Missionaries of St. Charles Borromeo, commonly known as the Scalabrinian Fathers and the Missionary Sisters of St. Charles. These two congregations are now present all over the world and continue to help immigrants. He was beatified by Pope John Paul II in 1907. Responding to a request from the Scalabrinians and bishop conferences around the world, Pope Francis dispensed with the usual canonization requirement of a miracle attributed to his intercession having occurred after beatification. Sister Lina Guzzo said of Scalabrini, "He rolled up his sleeves and took on in his person and in his heart, those who were lost and rejected. The Pope is canonizing him because he wants to give father to migrants."
182. "Why the Pope."
183. Vecoli, "Prelates and Peasants," 255.
184. Francesoni, *History of the Scalabrinian Congregation* 4:17. His entire letter is from this section.

6. Evolution of Two North End Churches

185. Devas, *Life of St. Leonard*. St. Leonard was born in 1676 in Genoa in Port-Maurice. His father was in the Genoese Merchant Service, a ship captain. He was an only child. His mother died shortly after he was born. His father remarried and sent him to Rome to live with a rich uncle, Augustin Casanova, at age thirteen. The goal was that he would study medicine and become a doctor. When he chose instead to become a priest, his rich uncle stopped supporting him and kicked him out, leaving him homeless. His father consented to his priesthood, and he became a Franciscan friar at age twenty-one. He took the name Leonard in memory of Leonard Ponzetti, a distant relative who had given him shelter when he was homeless. St. Leonard was

known for his missions to the masses, his retreats to the few and his personal letters of spiritual direction. His mission work started in 1708, when he was thirty-two, and continued for forty-three years until his death in November 1751. The erection of the Stations of the Cross was an invariable feature in his missions. The erection of the Stations of the Cross in Rome's Coliseum in December 1750 was his last great work in Rome. He was beatified by Pope Pius VI in 1796 and canonized by Pope Pius IX in 1867.

186. Many of the Irish parishioners worshipped at St. Leonard's because they were members of the Third Order. St. Francis of Assisi preached that many married men and women wanted to join the First Order (friars) or Second Order (nuns) but doing so was incompatible with their state of life. Thus, Francis found a middle way and in 1221 made them members of the Franciscan Third Order. Third Order Seculars do not wear religious habits, take vows or live in religious communities, but they profess to live out the Gospel life and commit themselves to that life. In 1978, the Third Order was recognized by Pope Paul VI, and the name was changed to the Secular Franciscan Order. At one time, St. Leonard's had a Third Order membership of over two thousand, becoming one of the most important Third Order fraternities in this country. See La Conte, "Catholic Church and the Italian Immigrant."

187. Lord and Harrington, *History of the Archdiocese*, 224.

188. This chapel was led by Father William Taylor, who was famous as a preacher. Father Taylor was born in Richmond, Virginia, in 1793 and went to sea at age seven. After a religious experience in 1811, Taylor decided to become a preacher. The War of 1812 postponed his plans. In 1814, he settled in Saugus and made his life peddling tin and iron wares and began preaching. In 1828 he moved to Boston—the same year the Port Society of Boston was organized by a company of members of the Methodist-Episcopal Church. At the first annual meeting of the society, it was decided that the first work to be done was the establishment of a Seaman's Bethel to provide worship for Boston's many sailors. In 1830 and 1831, Father Taylor went on an organized tour of the southern states and raised money. He returned to Boston with $21,000. In 1833, Bethel was completed at the cost of $24,000. Jenny Lind, Walt Whitman and Charles Dickens came to hear him preach. It is said he was the inspiration for Father Mapple in Melville's *Moby Dick*. Seaman's Aid Society was also founded to provide relief for seaman and their families. Father Taylor died in 1876. The building operated as Bethel until 1884, when it was acquired by the Saint Mark Society.

189. Bacigalupo, "Some Religious Aspects."

190. Martellone, *Una Little Italy*.

191. Ferraiuolo, *Religious Festive Practices*, 56.

192. Francesconi, *History of the Scalabrinian Congregation.* A member of the Sacra Congregegazione de Propaganda Fide, to Bishop Scalabrini, dated September 8, 1888.
193. DeMarco, *Ethnics & Enclaves*, chapter 4.
194. Ferraiuolo, *Religious Festive Practices*, 74–82.
195. Ibid., 74–82. Also referencing Barth, *Ethnic Groups and Boundaries.*
196. St. Stephen's Church was designed by the famous architect Charles Bulfinch. Rose Fitzgerald Kennedy was baptized at St. Stephen's, and her funeral Mass was held there.

7. Feasts

The fundamental source material for this chapter is Augusto Ferraiuolo's book *Religious Festive Practices in Boston's North End: Ephemeral Identities in an Italian American Community.*

197. Vecoli, "Prelates and Peasants," 268.
198. Ibid.
199. Gambera, *Migrant Missionary Story*, 157.
200. Ferraiuolo, *Religious Festive Practices*, chapter 3.
201. Durkheim, *Elementary Forms of Religious Life*, 64.
202. Ferraiuolo, *Religious Festive Practices*, chapter 4.
203. Ibid.
204. Durkheim, *Elementary Forms of Religious Life*, quoting Alexander, Geisen and Mast, *Social Performance*, 20–30.
205. Society of the Madonna Della Cava, www.madonnadellacava.com.
206. Ferraiuolo, *Religious Festive Practices*, 161–65.

8. Gentrification and the Future of the North End

Fundamental source materials for this chapter include Thomas O'Connor's book *Building a New Boston: Politics and Urban Renewal, 1950–1970.*

207. Dallin also sculpted the *Appeal to the Great Spirit* at the Museum of Fine Arts and the Anne Hutchinson statue located at the statehouse.
208. O'Connor, *Building a New Boston*, 125–26; Gans, *Urban Villagers*, 282.

209. O'Connor, *Building a New Boston*, xiii.

210. Ibid., 84–86.

211. Ferraiuolo, *Religious Festive Practices*, 18.

212. Ibid., 16.

213. O'Connor, *Building a New Boston*, xiii.

214. Giovannini, "Boston Waterfront."

215. O'Connor, *Building a New Boston*, 211; *Boston Globe*, January 9, 1964.

216. O'Connor, *Building a New Boston*, 212, quoting an undated letter of Edward Logue to Joseph A. Langone Jr., 58 Merrimac Street, Boston, Collins Papers Box 247; *Boston Herald*, May 26, 1984.

217. Giovannini, "Boston Waterfront."

218. Ferraiuolo, *Religious Festive Practices*, 21.

219. Giovannini, "Boston Waterfront."

220. Ferraiuoio, *Religious Festive Practices*, 74.

BIBLIOGRAPHY

Books, Chapters and Scholarly Articles

Agnew, W.H. "Pastoral Care of Italian Children in America." *Ecclesiastical Review* 48 (March 1913): 257–67.

Alexander, Jeffrey C., Bernhard Geisen and Jason L. Mast, eds. *Social Performance: Symbolic Action, Cultural Pragmatics and Ritual*. New York: Cambridge University Press, 1990.

Allison, Robert J. *A Short History of Boston*. Carlisle, MA: Commonwealth Editions, 2015.

Amore, B. *An Italian American Odyssey: Life line—filo della vita: Through Ellis Island and Beyond*. New York: Center for Migration Studies, 2006.

Armstrong, William H. *Father Taylor, Boston's Sailor Preacher: As Seen and Heard by His Contemporaries*. Self-published, Amazon, 2020.

Bacigalupo, Leonard, OFM. *The Franciscans and Italian Immigration to America*. New York: Mount Alvernia Friary, 1995.

———. "Some Religious Aspects Involving the Interaction of the Italians and the Irish." In *Italians and Irish in America: Proceedings of the Sixteenth Annual Conference of the Italian Historical Association*, edited by Francis X. Femminella. Staten Island, NY: Italian Historical Association, 1986.

Barr, Nancy Verde. *We Called It Macaroni: An American Heritage of Southern Italian Cooking*. New York: Knopf, 1990.

Barth, Fredrik, ed. *Ethnic Groups and Boundaries: The Social Organization of Cultural Differences.* London: George Allen & Unwin, 1969.

Blum, John M. "Review of *Henry Cabot Lodge: A Biography,* by John A. Garraty." *American Historical Review* 59, no. 3 (April 1954): 654–56.

Brown, Mary. "Early Twentieth Century Deportation and the Resistance." Center for Migration Studies. July 31, 2017. https://cmsny.org.

Brown, Mary Elizabeth. "The Theory and Practice of Language in Scalabrinian Parishes for Italian Immigrants in the United States, 1887–1933." *U.S. Catholic Historian* 33, no. 3 (2015): 51–68.

Browne, Henry J. "Catholicism in the United States." In *Religion in American Life,* vol. 1, edited by James Ward Smith and A. Leonard Jamison. Princeton, NJ: Princeton University Press, 1961.

Cannato, Vincent J. "Immigration and the Brahmins: An Influx of Undesirables at the End of the Nineteenth Century Hit Boston Elites Rather Hard." *Humanities* 30, no. 3 (May/June 2009).

Carey, Patrick. "The Laity's Understanding of the Trustee System, 1785–1855." *Catholic Historical Review* 64, no. 3 (July 1978): 357–76.

Carey, Patrick W. *People, Priests and Prelates: Ecclesiastical Democracy and the Tensions of Trusteeism.* Notre Dame, IN: University of Notre Dame Press, 1987.

Carr, John Foster. *The Guide to the United States for the Immigrant Italian.* New York: Doubleday, Page, 1911.

Chand, Rakashi. "Immigrants Needing Protection From Themselves? The Padrone System in Boston's North End." *The Beehive,* Massachusetts Historical Society, 2016. https://www.masshist.org.

"Chapter 10: The Italian Society of St. Raphael in Boston, 1902–1906." *Center for Migration Studies Special Issues* 16, no. 1 (January 2000): 202–27.

Cinel, Dino. *From Italy to San Francisco: The Immigrant Experience.* Stanford, CA: Stanford University Press, 1982.

Commager, Henry Steele. *The American Mind: An Interpretation of American Thought and Character Since the 1880s.* New Haven, CT: Yale University Press, 1959.

Commonwealth of Massachusetts. *The Problem of Immigration in Massachusetts.* Report of the Commission on Immigration. 1914. House No. 2300. Boston: Wright & Potter Printing Co., 1914.

Compston, Christine, Stephen Senge and Walter McDonald. *Rewarding Work: A History of North Bennet Street School.* Boston: North Bennet Street School, 2018.

Cunsolo, Ronald S. "Italian Emigration and Its Effect on the Rise of Nationalism." *Italian Americana* 12, no. 1 (1993): 62–73.

D'Amato, Gaetano. "The Black Hand Myth." *The North American Review* 187, no. 629 (April 1908): 545–49.

Darby, Mary. "In Ponzi We Trust." *Smithsonian Magazine*, December 1998.

Dash, Mike. *The First Family: Terror, Extortion, Revenge, Murder and the Birth of the American Mafia.* New York: Ballantine Books, 2009.

DeMarco, William. *Ethnics & Enclaves: Boston's Italian North End.* Ann Arbor, MI: Umi Research Press, 1981.

Devas, Dominic. *Life of St. Leonard of Port-Maurice: O.F.M. (1676–1751).* Whitefish, MT: Kessinger Publishing, 1920.

Dichtl, John R. *Frontiers of Faith: Bringing Catholicism to the West in the Early Republic.* Lexington: University of Kentucky Press, 2008.

Dos Passos, John. *Facing the Chair: Story of the Americanization of Two Foreign Born Workmen.* Boston: Sacco-Vanzetti Defense Committee, 1927.

———. "They Are Dead Now: Eulogy for Sacco and Vanzetti." *New Masses*, October 1927.

Dunne, Edmund M. "The Church and the Immigrant." In *Catholic Builders of the Nation*, vol. 2, edited by C.E. McGuire, 1–15. Boston: Continental Press, 1923.

Durkheim, Emile. *The Elementary Forms of Religious Life.* Translated by Carol Cosman. Oxford: Oxford University Press, 2001.

Elle, Lawrence. *Not So Long Ago: Oral Histories of Older Bostonians.* Boston: Mayor's Office of Community Schools, 1980.

Femminella, Francis X., ed. *Italians and Irish in America: Proceedings of the Sixteenth Annual Conference of the Italian Historical Association.* Staten Island, NY: Italian Historical Association, 1986.

Ferraiuolo, Augusto. "Boston's North End: Negotiating Identity in an Italian American Neighborhood." *Western Folklore* 65, no. 3 (Summer 2006): 263–302.

———. *Religious Festive Practices in Boston's North End: Ephemeral Identities in an Italian American Community.* Albany: SUNY Press, 2009.

Francesconi, Mario, CS. "Internal History of the Congregation (1896–1919)." In *History of the Scalabrinian Congregation*, vol. 4, translated by Martino Bortolazzo, CS. Province of St. Charles Borromeo Missionaries of Saint Charles–Scalabrinians; Provincial Archives Center for Migration Studies (CMS); Scalabrini International Migration Network (SIMN), 1983.

———. "Letters of Bishop Scalabrini from the United States (July–November 1901)." In *History of the Scalabrinian Congregation*, vol. 4, translated by Martino Bortolazzo, CS. Province of St. Charles Borromeo

Missionaries of Saint Charles–Scalabrinians; Provincial Archives Center for Migration Studies (CMS); Scalabrini International Migration Network (SIMN), 1983.

———. "Missions in North America (1895–1919)." In *History of the Scalabrinian Congregation*, vol. 4, translated by Martino Bortolazzo, CW. Province of St. Charles Borromeo Missionaries of Saint Charles–Scalabrinians; Provincial Archives Center for Migration Studies (CMS); Scalabrini International Migration Network (SIMN), 1983.

Frankfurter, Felix. *The Case for Sacco and Vanzetti: A Critical Analysis for Lawyers and Laymen.* Boston: Little Brown & Company, 1927.

Gambera, Giacomo. *A Migrant Missionary Story: The Autobiography of Giacomo Gambera.* Translated by Thomas Carlesimo, CS. New York: Center for Migration Studies, 1994.

Gamm, Gerald. *Urban Exodus: Why the Jews Left Boston and the Catholics Stayed.* Cambridge, MA: Harvard University Press, 1999.

Gans, Herbert. *The Urban Villagers: Group and Class in the Life of Italian Americans.* New York: Free Press, 1982.

Giamatti, A. Bartlett. "Commentary." In *The Italian Americans*, edited by Alan Schoener. New York: MacMillan Press, 1987.

Goldfield, Alex R. *The North End: A Brief History of Boston's Oldest Neighborhood.* Charleston, SC: The History Press, 2009.

Jacobs, Jane. *The Death and Life of Great American Cities.* New York: Vintage, 1992.

Janjevic, Darko. "Catholic Church Was 'Inconsistent' with the Mafia." Deutsche Welle (DW). December 11, 2016. https://www.dw.com.

Killinger, Charles L. *The History of Italy.* Westport, CT: Greenwood Press, 2002.

Kiriakova, Maria. "Wall Street Bombing of 1920." Encyclopedia Britannica, 2022. https://www.britannica.com.

Langone, Fred. *The North End: Where It All Began.* Self-published, 1992.

Lodge, Henry Cabot. "The Restriction of Immigration." *The North American Review* 152, no. 410 (January 1891): 27–36.

Lord, Section, and Edward T. Harrington. *History of the Archdiocese of Boston, 1604–1942.* New York: Sheed & Ward, 1944.

Marraro, Howard R. *American Opinion on the Unification of Italy 1846–1861.* New York: Columbia University Press, 1932.

Martellone, Anna Maria. *Una Little Italy nell'Atene d'America. La Comunita Italiana di Boston dal 1800 al 1920.* Studio Sud, no. 6. Naples: Guida, 1973.

Merlino, Rossella. "Sicilian Mafia, Patron Saints and Religious Processions: The Consistent Face of an Ever-Changing Criminal Organization." *California Italian Studies* 5, no. 1 (2014). https://doi.org/10.5070/C351023579.

Molinari, Bennett R., and Richard C. Molinari. *Four Women (Quattro Donne): A North End Love Story*. Lulu Publishing Services, 2019.

Nelli, Humbert. *From Immigrants to Ethnics: Italian Americans*. Oxford, UK: Oxford University Press, 1983.

O'Connor, Thomas. *Boston Catholics: A History of the Church and Its People*. Boston: Northeastern University Press, 1998.

———. *Building a New Boston: Politics and Urban Renewal, 1950–1970*. Boston: Northeastern University Press, 1995.

Panunzio, Constantine. "Arriving in Boston (1902)." In *The Italian Americans*, edited by Allon Schoener. New York: Macmillan, 1987.

Pasto, James S. "Immigrants and Ethnics: Post World War II Italian Immigration and Boston's North End (1945–2016)." In *New Italian Migrations to the United States. Politics and History Since 1945*, vol. 1, edited by Laura E. Ruberto and Joseph Sciorra. Champaign: University of Illinois Press, 2017.

Ponzi, Charles. *The Rise and Fall of Mr. Ponzi*. Digital Mammouth Editions, originally published 1936. http://pnzi.com.

Pope-Obeda, Emily. "Expelling the Foreign-Born Menace: Immigrant Dissent, the Early Deportation State, and the First American Red Scare." *Journal of the Gilded Age and Progressive Era* 18, no. 1 (2019): 1–24. doi: 10.1017/S1537781418000592.

Puleo, Stephen. *The Boston Italians: A Story of Pride, Perseverance and Paesani from the Years of the Great Immigration to the Present Day*. Boston: Beacon Press, 2008.

Riccio, Anthony. *Boston's North End: Images and Recollections of an Italian-American Neighborhood*. Guilford, CT: Insider's Guide, 2006.

———. *Stories, Streets and Saints: Photographs and Oral Histories from Boston's North End*. Albany, NY: Excelsior Editions, 2022.

Sacco, Nicola, and Bartolomeo Vanzetti. *The Letters of Sacco and Vanzetti*. New York: Octagon Books, 1928.

Sammarco, Anthony Mitchell. *Boston's North End* (Images of America). Charleston, SC: Arcadia Publishing, 2004.

———. *Boston's North End* (Then and Now). Charleston, SC: Arcadia Publishing. 2007.

Schiavo, Giovanni. *Italian American History*. Vol. 2 of *The Italian Contribution to the Catholic Church in America*. New York: Vigo Press, 1949.

Schroth, Raymond. "Church in Crises—Analysis." *National Catholic Reporter* (Kansas City, MO), November 1, 2022.

Sweeney, Emily. *Gangland Boston: A Tour Through the Streets of Organized Crime*. Lanham, MD: National Book Network, 2018.

Todisco, Paula. *Boston's First Neighborhood: The North End.* Boston: Boston Public Library, 1976.

Van Hove, A. "Fabrica Ecclesiae." In *The Catholic Encyclopedia.* New York: Robert Appleton Company, 2022.

Vecoli, Rudolph J. "Prelates and Peasants: Italian Immigrants and the Catholic Church." *Journal of Social History* 2, no. 3 (Spring 1969): 217–68. http://www.jstor.org/stable/3786488.

Watson, Bruce. *Sacco and Vanzetti: The Men, The Murders, and the Judgment of Mankind.* New York: Viking Penguin, 2007.

Whyte, William Foote. "Race Conflicts in the North End of Boston." *New England Quarterly* 12, no. 4 (December 1939): 623.

―――. *Street Corner Society: The Social Structure of an Italian Slum.* Chicago: University of Chicago Press, 1943.

Woods, Robert A. *Americans in Progress: A Settlement Study.* Boston: Houghton Mifflin, 1903.

―――. "Notes on the Italians in Boston (1904)." In *The Italian in America: The Progressive View, 1891–1914*, edited by Lydio F. Tomasi. New York: Center for Migration Studies, 1978.

Master's Theses

Farmelant, Kristen P. "Trophies of Grace: Religious Conversion and Americanization in Boston's Immigrant Communities, 1890–1940." Master's thesis, Brown University, 2001.

La Conte, John, OFM. "The Catholic Church and the Italian Immigrant Colony in Boston." Master's thesis, Catholic University of America, 1968.

Piccoli, G. "Italian Immigration in the United States." Master's thesis, Duquesne University, 2014.

Puleo, Stephen. "From Italy to Boston's North End: Italian Immigration and Settlement, 1890–1910." Master's thesis, University of Massachusetts, 1994.

Articles

Bullard, F. Lauriston. "Proposed Reforms Echo of Sacco Case." *New York Times*, December 11, 1927.

Dello Russo, Jessica. "On a Goodly Square: Sacred Heart Italian Mission to Boston's North End." North End Waterfront. December 28, 2020. https://northendwaterfront.com.

Donati, Silvia. "Where to Find Italy in America: Boston's North End." *Italy Magazine*, 2016.

Dumanoksi, Dianne. "Revisiting the Beginnings of North End Gentrification in the 1970's." North End Waterfront. January 10, 2017. https://northendwaterfront.com.

Giovannini, Joseph. "Boston Waterfront: At 25, a Model Urban Renewal." *New York Times*, September 21, 1986.

Guarino, Christian Anthony. "The History of Saint Leonard Church: Part 1, Boston 'Welcomes' the Catholics." North End Waterfront. December 3, 2017. https://northendwaterfront.com.

———. "The History of Saint Leonard Church: Part 2, The Franciscans and a Growing Italian Community." North End Waterfront. December 20, 2017. https://northendwaterfront.com.

———. "The History of Saint Leonard Church: Part 3, A Neighborhood Church with A Global Impact." North End Waterfront. December 12, 2017. https://northendwaterfront.com.

Herwick, Edgar, III. "This Week in History: The Boston Post Takes Down Charles Ponzi." GBH, July 25, 2014. http://news.wgbh.org.

Hunt, Thomas. "New England (Patriarca) Mob Leaders." American Mafia, 2021. https://mafiahistory.us.

Kulina, Lydia. "What Jane Jacobs Missed About Boston's North End." Next City, 2019. https://nextcity.org.

Messick, Hank. "History of the Mafia in Boston and New England." Trivia Library, 1981. https://www.trivia-library.com.

Nichols, Guild. "Part 5: Boston's Little Italy, 1900–Today." Pastene. September 7, 2015. https://www.pastene.com.

Pope-Obeda, Emily. "This Deportation Business: 1920s and the Present." Against the Current, 2016. https://againstthecurrent.org.

Staples, Brent. "How Italians Became 'White.'" *New York Times*, October 12, 2019.

Traficante, Tony. "The Great Arrival and Dawn of Italian America." Italian Sons and Daughters in America. October 8, 2019. https://orderisda.org.

Tuttle, Mandy. "Italian Immigration to America and Boston's North End." Paul Revere House. April 24, 2020. www.paulreverehouse.org.

Websites and Other Resources

Dante Alighieri Society of Massachusetts (Cambridge, MA). www.dantemass.org.

North End Historical Society (Boston, MA). www.northendboston.org.

Saint Leonard's of Port-Maurice (Boston, MA). www.saintleonardchurchboston.org.

Feast Societies

Madonna Del Soccorso Society Fisherman's Club. www.fishermansfeast.com

Saint Agrippina Boston. www.saintagrippinaboston.com.

Saint Anthony's Feast. www.stanthonysfeast.com.

Saint Joseph Society. www.saintjosephsboston.com.

Santa Maria Di Anzano Procession. www.anzanoboston.com.

Society of the Madonna Della Cava. www.madonnadellacava.com.

ABOUT THE AUTHOR

Patricia M. Annino is an estate planning attorney in Boston with more than thirty years of experience serving the needs of families, individuals and closely held businesses. She is of Irish/Italian descent and lives in the North End with her husband. She has respect and admiration for her family's resilience and perseverance in their journey from Italy to Boston. When walking through the streets of the North End and attending Mass at St. Leonard's, she feels the deep connection to her Italian roots and marvels at how the soul of the Italian immigrant remains omnipresent in the enclave.